D0512391

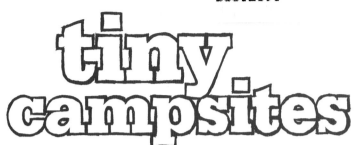

**Discover Britain's little
pockets of camping bliss**

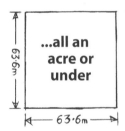

...all an
acre or
under

63·6m

63·6m

Dixe Wills

Tiny Campsites
Published in the United Kingdom in 2010 by
Punk Publishing Ltd
3 The Yard
Pegasus Place
London
SE11 5SD

www.punkpublishing.co.uk

A catalogue record of this book is available from the British Library.

ISBN 978-1-906889-06-7

10 9 8 7 6 5 4 3 2 1

For Carl, who taught me everything
I know about camping.

And for Mike, who didn't.

Contents

Introduction

'Man is small and, therefore, small is beautiful.'

So wrote the late philosopher-economist EF Schumacher, and I think it's fairly safe to assume that he had campsites uppermost in his mind when the notion came to him. Certainly, the tide of evidence backing up his assertion is irresistible: whether on a farm, by the sea, behind a pub, beside a river, on a tiny island or even next to a museum, a small campsite will always triumph over a large one in the same way that a cosy boutique will ever prevail over a warehouse-like chain store. It's a matter of soul.

It was an incident that occurred in the summer of 2001 that convinced me of the truth of Schumacher's maxim. I'd just enjoyed a very pleasant day cycling around Dartmoor. I hadn't booked anywhere for the night so, with evening drawing on, I made for a campsite marked on my OS map. Hauling myself over one last hill the trees parted and I looked down on the modest slice of Devon that was to be my home for the night. But at the sight of it my little heart sank. The bijou glade of my imaginings was, in reality, a huge commercial site that appeared to have been styled after a particularly unfortunate internment camp – nothing but rows of static caravans and expanses of tarmac. I stopped at the bottom of the hill and took out my map: no other campsites for miles and miles.

I was just beginning to resign myself to my fate when a sign on a tree caught my eye. Handwritten and fastened to the trunk by drawing pins, it bore the simple one-word legend 'Camping', with an arrow pointing right. Ten minutes later I was putting my tent up on the back lawn of a gorgeous farmhouse. Birds flitted around me, an apple tree proffered the possibility of free pudding and my pitch was surrounded on three sides by flowerbeds bursting with colour – it was very heaven. And still is, in fact – if you want to find out yourself, it's Sweet Meadows (p30).

I spend a great deal of my time wandering around Britain (it's okay, I'm a travel writer, it's what we do) and for roughly two months a year I'm under canvas, so I've stumbled across a good number of tiny campsites over the years. Sadly, a few have aped some of the worst examples of their larger brethren by being little more than glorified car parks. However, a lot more have turned out to be cracking little places that have gladdened my soul on arrival, and where I've left a little bit of my heart on departure (it's a disgusting habit, I know, but I'm otherwise very tidy).

It was when I started looking for a book on the nation's best diminutive campsites that the problems began. It quickly became apparent that no such guide existed and that if I wanted one I would have to write it myself. And so it was that I ended up cycling over 2,000 miles in a (let's face it, highly enjoyable) bid to winkle out the finest campsites in Britain of an acre or under. I was also keen to include some of the really useful information that most camping books leave out, such as the opening times of the nearest shop and what coins, if any, you need for the showers. After all, there's nothing like arriving at a remote site hungry and foodless because you didn't know that Wednesday was early closing, or finding yourself stripped and ready for action only to discover that you haven't a single 20p piece to your name.

Anyway, since you're probably only reading this introduction if you're at a campsite right now and have forgotten to bring along any other reading material with you, I shall end here – first, by hoping you derive as much pleasure from visiting the sites in this book as I have, and then by reminding you that, if you're reading this at Cedar Gables (p68), Quarryfield (p108), Silver Birches (p162) or Badrallach (p178) you're in luck – they've all got little libraries.

Dixe Wills

Top Tips

Help! What should I pack?

If you're new to camping and live in mortal fear of turning up at some remote campsite having forgotten a vital item of equipment, then panic no more. Aside from a tent, sleeping bag and mat, spare clothes (including waterproofs) and toiletries, these are the essentials to pop in your rucksack:

- cooking equipment (stove, fuel, lighter, pan, cutlery, mug, bowl)
- food (couscous is brilliant – avoid tins and anything ambitious)
- tea bags (it's not camping otherwise)
- tools (Swiss Army knife, head torch, map and compass)
- frisbee (entertainment and plate rolled into one)
- milk powder (great when far from supplies of fresh milk)
- loo roll (handy emergency pillow, among other uses)
- water bottle
- basic first aid kit

Camping is about being free and easy, so try not to pack the kitchen sink (if you really need one, you can fashion one out of twigs when you get there).

Pitching your tent

Everyone who's been camping for any length of time has a camping disaster story to tell: a tent that leaked, a tent that got washed away, a tent that got blown away or a tent that defied all attempts to be erected in the first place. However, there's no reason why any of these calamities should necessary befall you. If you follow a few simple rules, you may never find

yourself fighting with a guy rope in the pouring rain at two o'clock in the morning. Unless, of course, that's what you like to do.

- Always have a practice go at putting up a new tent before you travel to check that you can do it and all its parts are in situ.
- It may seem like stating the obvious, but do read the instructions carefully while pitching your tent. Following your instincts rather than the little pictures on the stuff sack may be more fun at first but is a course of action that is likely to end badly, if not in tears.
- In blustery weather, pitch your tent with its smaller end directly into the wind. Use all the guy ropes available, and weigh each peg down with a large stone (or similar) to anchor it.
- Insert pegs so they point outwards from the tent at roughly 45 degrees.
- Don't let anything inside your tent push the inner compartment on to the flysheet as this will let water into the tent.
- Keep your tent ventilated to avoid condensation building up inside.

Midges

The Biting Midge, a member of the mighty *Ceratopogonidae* family, is not only the summer curse of the Scottish Highlands, but often makes its way south as far as northern England. However, if you forget to pack the anti-midge lotion or fail to eat Marmite every day for a fortnight beforehand (yes, it works – no pest enjoys supping Marmite-tainted blood), don't worry, as there are still plenty of ways to keep yourself bite-free:

- Wear white or light-coloured clothing.
- Stay in the sun rather than shade.
- Avoid sitting outside in the early morning or late evening.
- Get yourself into a breeze or create your own by keeping on the move.

How to Use this Book

Campsite tariffs – an enigma for our times

Visit a dozen campsites and the likelihood is that they'll have 12 different ways of charging customers. Some quote a price per person; others per unit; still others per pitch, while some employ arcane algebraic formulae where x = *the cubic volume of the tent multiplied by π, and* y = *the number of campers divided by the square root of their IQ*. Then there are discounts for children, for those arriving by public transport; extra charges for dogs, cars, awnings and electric hook-ups; the list goes on...

So, to simplify matters, in this book the cost of each campsite is given in £ signs to indicate roughly what you can expect to pay if you are:

• A solo backpacker/cyclist (BP) with a small tent
• A couple: two people sharing a medium-sized tent
• A family: two adults and two children sharing a large tent

£	=	Up to £5
££	=	Up to £10
£££	=	Up to £15
££££	=	Up to £20
£££££	=	Over £20

So, if the cost at Happy Clappy Farm is quoted as: BP £, Couple ££, Family ££££, it means that a backpacker would normally pay less than £5; a couple would fork out somewhere between a fiver and a tenner between them; while a family would be charged £15 to £20. Please note, however, that at some campsites, campervanners and caravanners may pay extra, especially if they want some electricity too.

All the campsites in this book supply free drinking water, usually from a conveniently placed standpipe.

Symbols

▲ tents		🚐 vintage VW campervans only	
🚌 all campervans		🚐 caravans	

Tiny Campsites' Rating		Friendliness	
✳	Great	☺	Welcoming
✳✳	Fantastic	☺☺	Highly convivial
✳✳✳	Drop dead gorgeous	☺☺☺	Chums for life

Out and About recommendations are, as a general rule, listed in order of the author's (admittedly subjective) preference.

Key to abbreviations:

FACILITIES	OUT AND ABOUT
4U = 4 unisex toilets/showers	7D = 7 days a week
1M = 1 men's toilet/shower	U14 = under the age of 14
2W = 2 ladies' toilets/showers	News-tob-con = newsagent-
CDP = chemical disposal point	tobacconist-confectioner
4WD = 4-wheel-drive vehicle	PO = post office
max. = maximum of	w/e = weekend
min. = minutes	BH = bank holiday
	pp = per person
	NT site = National Trust website,
	www.nationaltrust.org.uk

Top Five

A breathtaking vista of the Cornish coast, a picturesque village and harbour to explore, a maximum of 12 campers on site, and a scrummy breakfast brought to your tent each morning. Absolute heaven.

Think of the finest view of the countryside imaginable and then double it. Double it again and you've got the view from Park Farm. That's a cool 50 miles to Tan Hill and the Yorkshire Dales, and everything in between is one generous dollop of gorgeous English countryside. Pack your watercolours.

Think of Middle Ninfa, with its private pitches high up on the edge of the Brecon Beacons, as your very own Welsh bolt-hole. And should you ever tire of the panoramic view you can always avail yourself of the croquet lawn.

Not so much a campsite as the best back garden you've ever spent the night in. There's room for just four tents in this miniature Highland glade – the rest is taken up by hammocks, red squirrels and, yes, loads of lazy ducks...

Tucked beneath a mountain on the north-west coast of Scotland, Badrallach makes other off-the-beaten-track campsites look positively urban. Bring your sea legs too: there are kayaks for hire and a loch waiting to be explored.

Campsites Sorted

The easy way to choose your site

TENTS ONLY

No 2 Dennis Farm
8 Spyway Inn
9 California Cottage
13 Daneway Inn
14 Abbey Home
Farm Glade
16 Rushey Lock
17 Pinkhill Lock
18 Cookham Lock
19 Gumber Farm
20 Evergreen Farm
21 Foxhole Bottom
27 The Jolly Sailor
40 Quarryfield
44 Piel Island
49 Hollins Farm
50 Park Farm
57 Lone Wolf
58 Middle Ninfa Farm
59 Little Oasis
70 The Lazy Duck

KIDS

2 Dennis Farm
4 Little Wenfork
10 Parish Lantern
20 Evergreen Farm
25 Walton Hall Museum
26 Spencer's Farm Shop
30 Brickyard Farm
33 The Beeches
35 The Bridge Inn
36 Nicholson Farm
44 Piel Island
45 Birchbank Farm
46 Dalegarth
48 Wold Farm
49 Hollins Farm
55 Glyn-Coch
Craft Centre
56 Eastern Slade Farm
58 Middle Ninfa Farm
64 Gwersyll Maes-y-Bryn
66 Treheli Farm

WALKERS

1 Broad Meadow House
5 Sweet Meadows
6 Millslade
9 California Cottage
11 Church Farm
12 Rectory Farm
16 Rushey Lock
17 Pinkhill Lock
18 Cookham Lock
19 Gumber Farm
20 Evergreen Farm
21 Foxhole Bottom
29 Potton Hall
31 Scaldbeck Cottage
32 Braham Farm
35 The Bridge Inn
37 The Buzzards
40 Quarryfield
41 The Wild Boar Inn
42 Rowan Bank
43 Crawshaw Farm
45 Birchbank Farm
46 Dalegarth
47 Elmtree Farm
48 Wold Farm
49 Hollins Farm
50 Park Farm
51 Highside Farm
52 The Old Vicarage
53 Rye Hill Farm
54 Porthllisky Farm
58 Middle Ninfa Farm
59 Little Oasis
60 Castle Inn
61 Radnors End
63 Ty Maen Farm
65 Silver Birches
66 Treheli Farm
70 The Lazy Duck
72 Badrallach

CYCLISTS

2 Dennis Farm
7 Bridge Farm
11 Church Farm
15 Lyneham Lake
20 Evergreen Farm
35 The Bridge Inn
36 Nicholson Farm
37 The Buzzards
41 The Wild Boar Inn
43 Crawshaw Farm
47 Elmtree Farm
50 Park Farm
52 The Old Vicarage
60 Castle Inn
61 Radnors End
67 The Ken Bridge Hotel
68 Glenmidge Smithy
70 The Lazy Duck

WILD

13 Daneway Inn
14 Abbey Home
Farm Glade
20 Evergreen Farm
23 Welsummer
24 Woodland Farm
44 Piel Island
57 Lone Wolf
58 Middle Ninfa Farm

PUBS

8 Spyway Inn
10 Parish Lantern
13 Daneway Inn
27 The Jolly Sailor
34 The Green Man
35 The Bridge Inn
41 The Wild Boar Inn
44 Piel Island
60 Castle Inn
67 The Ken Bridge Hotel
74 Halladale Inn

COASTAL

1 Broad Meadow House
2 Dennis Farm
9 California Cottage
21 Foxhole Bottom
27 The Jolly Sailor
31 Scaldbeck Cottage
44 Piel Island
47 Elmtree Farm
54 Porthllisky Farm
56 Eastern Slade Farm
66 Treheli Farm
69 Balmeanach Park
72 Badrallach
73 Inver
74 Halladale Inn
75 Eilean Fraoich

WATERSIDE

2 Dennis Farm
6 Millslade
15 Lyneham Lake
16 Rushey Lock
17 Pinkhill Lock
18 Cookham Lock
34 The Green Man
35 The Bridge Inn
39 Four Oaks
44 Piel Island
45 Birchbank Farm
46 Dalegarth
57 Lone Wolf
62 Trericket Mill
67 The Ken Bridge Hotel
70 The Lazy Duck
71 The Wee Camp Site
72 Badrallach

CAMPFIRES

4 Little Wenfork
5 Sweet Meadows
6 Millslade
9 California Cottage
11 Church Farm
14 Abbey Home
  Farm Glade
19 Gumber Farm
20 Evergreen Farm
23 Welsummer
24 Woodland Farm

26 Spencer's Farm Shop
31 Scaldbeck Cottage
39 Four Oaks
49 Hollins Farm
50 Park Farm
57 Lone Wolf
58 Middle Ninfa Farm
59 Little Oasis
62 Trericket Mill
66 Treheli Farm
72 Badrallach

EASY PUBLIC TRANSPORT

2 Dennis Farm
15 Lyneham Lake
26 Spencer's Farm Shop
31 Scaldbeck Cottage
34 The Green Man
37 The Buzzards
50 Park Farm
63 Ty Maen Farm

HIDEAWAY

5 Sweet Meadows
13 Daneway Inn
14 Abbey Home
  Farm Glade
19 Gumber Farm
20 Evergreen Farm
28 High House Fruit Farm
29 Potton Hall
32 Braham Farm
37 The Buzzards
39 Four Oaks
43 Crawshaw Farm
45 Birchbank Farm
48 Wold Farm
50 Park Farm
51 Highside Farm
55 Glyn-Coch
  Craft Centre
58 Middle Ninfa Farm
65 Silver Birches

VIEWS

1 Broad Meadow House
2 Dennis Farm
3 Scadghill Farm
4 Little Wenfork

7 Bridge Farm
8 Spyway Inn
11 Church Farm
32 Braham Farm
36 Nicholson Farm
38 Forestside Farm
41 The Wild Boar Inn
42 Rowan Bank
43 Crawshaw Farm
44 Piel Island
45 Birchbank Farm
49 Hollins Farm
50 Park Farm
51 Highside Farm
53 Rye Hill Farm
54 Porthllisky Farm
56 Eastern Slade Farm
58 Middle Ninfa Farm
59 Little Oasis
61 Radnors End
64 Gwersyll Maes-y-Bryn
65 Silver Birches
66 Treheli Farm
70 The Lazy Duck
71 The Wee Camp Site
72 Badrallach
73 Inver
74 Halladale Inn

WATER SPORTS

1 Broad Meadow House
2 Dennis Farm
3 Scadghill Farm
9 California Cottage
16 Rushey Lock
17 Pinkhill Lock
18 Cookham Lock
22 Cedar Gables
27 The Jolly Sailor
31 Scaldbeck Cottage
34 The Green Man
61 Radnors End
62 Trericket Mill
67 The Ken Bridge Hotel
72 Badrallach
74 Halladale Inn

South-West England

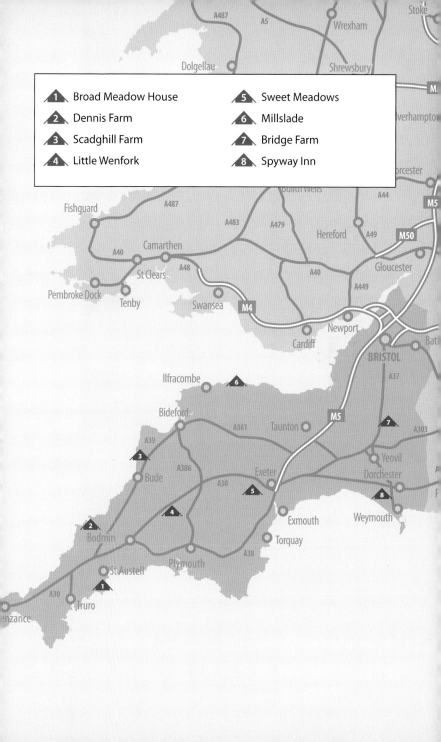

1. Broad Meadow House
2. Dennis Farm
3. Scadghill Farm
4. Little Wenfork
5. Sweet Meadows
6. Millslade
7. Bridge Farm
8. Spyway Inn

1 Broad Meadow House

Quay Road
Charlestown
St Austell
Cornwall
PL25 3NX

Deb Best
01726 76636
stay@broadmeadowhouse.co.uk
www.broadmeadowhouse.co.uk
Landranger: 200 (SX 040 516)

THE BASICS
Size: ⁴/₅ acre.
Pitches: Max. 12 people on site (0 hard standing).
Terrain: Slopey, but all pitches level.
Shelter: From all sides but seaward.
View: The shoreline of St Austell Bay.
Waterside: Cliffs 100 metres.
Electric hook-ups: 4.
Noise/Light/Olfactory pollution: None.

THE FACILITIES
Loos: 1U. **Showers**: 1U (free).
Other facilities: Washing-up sink, mini fridge & freezer, wi-fi, recharging point.
Stuff for children: A separate field for games.
Recycling: Everything.

THE RULES
Dogs: If well behaved and on leads.
Fires: No open fires; BBQs off grass (granite blocks available). **Other**: Only campervans accepted are small vintage VW vans.

PUB LIFE
Pier House Hotel (free house), Charlestown (200 metres) – harbourside snug bar with highly recommended food and live entertainment Sat evenings; open Mon–Thur 11:30am–2:30pm & 6–11pm, Fri–Sat till midnight, Sun 12–2:30pm & 6–11pm; food served 6–9:30pm 7D; 01726 67955; www.pierhousehotel.com.

SHOP
Carlyon Bay PO (1 mile via coastal path) – quite basic supplies; open Mon–Fri 7am–5:30pm, Sat till 5pm, Sun 8am–noon; 01726 812728.

THERE AND AWAY
Train station: St Austell (1½ miles) – Plymouth to Penzance line. The Western Greyhound (www.westerngreyhound.com) bus no. 525 runs hourly from St Austell to Charlestown.

OUT AND ABOUT
Charlestown Shipwreck & Heritage Centre (50 metres) – 'the largest collection of shipwreck artefacts in Britain'; adult £5.80, child £2.90, U10 free; open daily March to October 10am–5pm; 01726 69897; www.shipwreckcharlestown.com.
Eden Project, Bodelva (4 miles – footpath route maps from campsite available) – one millennium project that appears to have been a great success. Each football-like biome takes you into a different region in the world, and there are large discounts if you arrive by foot or bicycle (see prices in brackets); adult £16 (£12), child £5 (free), family £38 (£24); open daily April to October 9am (gates open at 10am)–6pm (last entry 4:30pm) see website for winter opening hours; 01726 811911; www.edenproject.com.

open	May to September (weather dependent)
tiny campsites' rating	✷ ✷ ✷
friendliness	☺ ☺ ☺
cost	BP ££, Couple ££££, Family £££££

Walk past Charlestown's museum and along the short cul-de-sac behind it and you'd be forgiven for being sceptical about there being a campsite here at all, let alone one of the tastiest in the country. However, just beyond the final house, a gate opens up to a couple of tiny fields that command fabulous views out to sea and along the shoreline towards Black Head, the tip of a headland sporting the golden flash of a wheat field on its back.

Broad Meadow (Was it ever broad? Ancient sepia photos suggest not.) has two geese, a 'posh shed', three permanent tents and plenty of space for people who'd rather bring their own. Since the owners limit the number of campers on site to a mere dozen, you get the distinct feeling of being one of an incredibly privileged few. This is especially true if you order a delicious breakfast basket (including freshly made smoothie) to be brought to your tent in the morning.

Basking sharks and grey seals are sometimes spotted in the bay (just ask to borrow the telescope) while peregrine falcons, sparrowhawks and buzzards contest the air space above. Swallows, sensibly, prefer to skim the surface of the field and are so used to company that they come quite close to feed.

In tiny Charlestown there's some easy coasteering to be had; a gig club (www.charlestown.org.uk) that allows beginners to have a go at rowing on novice nights (Wednesdays); and, for those who want to go it alone, sea kayaks and other water vessels can be hired (www.charlestownwatersports.com).

Dennis Lane
Padstow
Cornwall
PL28 8DR

Ann and Barry Harris
01841 533513
Landranger: 200 (SW 920 743)

THE BASICS

Size: ⅗ acre.
Pitches: 24 (0 hard standing).
Terrain: Sloping with some level pitches.
Shelter: On 2 sides.
View: Across the Camel Estuary to the village of Rock.
Waterside: Yes.
Electric hook-ups: No.
Noise/Light/Olfactory pollution: The globular yellow blobs of the Padstow street lights; the salty tang of seaweed at low tide.

THE FACILITIES

Loos: 3M 4W. **Showers**: 2U & 1 disabled/family (40p tokens 'for 5 min.').
Other facilities: Washing machine, tumble-dryer, 3 washing-up areas, external shower for surfers, CDP; gas bottles for sale; ice blocks can be hired for 40p.
Stuff for children: Field for games.
Recycling: No.

THE RULES

Dogs: On leads.
Fires: No open fires; concrete blocks available for BBQs.
Other: No large groups.

PUB LIFE

Golden Lion (free house), Lanadwell Street, Padstow (¾ mile) – dating back to the 14th century and possessor of the 'Obby 'Oss that is paraded through town every May Day to the accompaniment of drums and accordions; open 11am–11pm 7D; food served Mon–Sat 12–2:30pm & 6:30–9pm, Sun 12–2pm & 6:30–9pm; 01841 532797; www.goldenlionpadstow.co.uk.

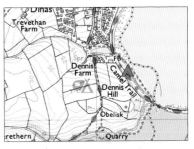

Or try the **Old Ship Hotel** (free house), Mill Square, Padstow (¾ mile) – a pub that does breakfasts if you've forgotten to pack your muesli; open 8:30am–11pm 7D; breakfast served till 10:30am, lunch/dinner 12–9:30pm; 01841 532357; www.oldshiphotel-padstow.co.uk.

SHOP

Spar, Middle Street, Padstow (¾ mile) – basics and off licence; open Mon–Sat 7am–8pm, Sun 8am–7pm; 01841 553400. There's a wide range of shops in town, too.

THERE AND AWAY

Train station: Bodmin Parkway (19 miles) – Exeter to Penzance line. There is a regular bus route between the station and Padstow – see main text.

OUT AND ABOUT

Camel Trail – see main text; free; always open; 01872 327310 (for free leaflet); www.sustrans.org.uk.
Padstow – there's more to the picturesque working port than the Rick Stein restaurant; www.padstowlive.com.

open	Whitsun Bank Holiday to mid September
tiny campsites' rating	★ ★ ★
friendliness	☺☺
cost	Cost: BP ££, Couple ££££, Family ££££

The first thing you learn when staying at Dennis Farm is that it's not the campsite called Dennis Cove. The two were once one, but have now split, with the much larger Dennis Cove on one side of the headland, and the diminutive Dennis Farm site – an isolated strip of coastal loveliness, free from crowds, madding or otherwise – on the other.

The view across the Camel Estuary, with its bobbing flotsam of yachts, canoes, power boats, windsurfers and water skiers, is as eye-pleasing and summery as a vista can be. The very best vantage points are at the far end of the site on a tiny plateau reserved for backpackers and cyclists.

The Camel Trail runs right through the site – you cross it to get to the smart loo block – taking cyclists, walkers and the occasional horse-rider to Padstow (½ mile) or, in the other direction, to Bodmin (10½ miles) via Wadebridge (4½ miles). The trail runs along a disused railway line, making it very flat and thus a hit with young families. All manner of bicycles, including tandems, can be hired very reasonably at Padstow Cycle Hire (½ mile; 01841 533533; www.padstowcyclehire.com).

Unusually (indeed, perhaps even uniquely), the campsite possesses four moorings and a slipway that can handle anything from small dinghies to 14-footers. If you'd rather arrive by land, however, the bus no. 555 runs direct from Bodmin Parkway railway station to Padstow (01637 871871; www.westerngreyhound.com).

Bude
Cornwall
EX23 9HN

Mr and Mrs SR Berrett
01288 352357
Landranger: 190 (SS 222 102)

THE BASICS
Size: ⅓ acre.
Pitches: 5 caravans and a variable number of tents (0 hard standing).
Terrain: Very gently sloping.
Shelter: Hedge to east and north.
View: Dartmoor, Bodmin Moor.
Waterside: No.
Electric hook-ups: No.
Noise/Light/Olfactory pollution: Cows' moos.

THE FACILITIES
Loos: 1U. **Showers**: 1U (2 x 10p for '6 min.').
Other facilities: CDP.
Stuff for children: No.
Recycling: Everything.

THE RULES
Dogs: On leads. **Fires**: No open fires; BBQs off ground. **Other**: No.

PUB LIFE
New Inn (free house), Kilkhampton (2½ miles) – a 15th-century pub with its own skittle alley (available September to May); open Mon–Fri 11am–3pm & 6–11pm, w/es 11am–11pm; food served 12–2pm & 6–9pm 7D; 01288 321488.

SHOP
Kilkhampton (2½ miles) runs to a **Londis** (convenience store; 8am–8pm 7D) and a **Spar** (convenience store and off licence; 8am–9pm 7D) as well as a fish-and-chip shop, a pizzeria, a PO and a toyshop.

THERE AND AWAY
Train station: Gunnislake (34 miles) – Gunnislake to Plymouth line. It's best to

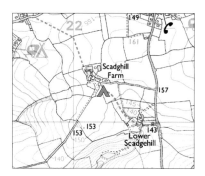

get a taxi from the station, as there are no direct bus services onwards.

OUT AND ABOUT
Bude (3½ miles) – a curious place: a seaside town that revolves around its river and canal, and yet has made its name as a surfers' paradise; www.visitbude.info.
Dinscott Tank & Military Collection, Stibb (1 mile) – all the military paraphernalia a testosterone-fuelled boy could wish for, plus the opportunity to ride in, or even drive, a tank; adult £4.50, U14 £3.50, U5 free; open June to September Mon–Sat 10am–5pm (see website for non-summer opening times); 01288 321556 & 07855 261169; www.tankdriving.net.

open	All year
tiny campsites' rating	★ ★
friendliness	☺☺☺
cost	BP ££, Couple ££, Family ££

Climb the hill from Bude up to Scadghill Farm under your own steam and it really whets your appetite for the view at the top. The panorama does not disappoint, laying before the eyes a feast of countryside spread out like a spectacularly wrinkled green tea-towel. Best of all, and high above everything else, stand what appear to be two hills. One turns out to be Bodmin Moor, some 20 miles away, while the other is Dartmoor, 25 miles to the south-east. It's difficult to believe that the former actually covers 100 square-miles, while the latter extends to a full 368; from Scadghill you feel you could scale them in one or two bounds, before breakfast if necessary.

The campsite is a quarter of a mile from the road along a farm track, thus ensuring that there is nothing to disturb the peace and quiet but the low moomur of cows. The facilities can be found around the back of a nearby bungalow lived in by Derek, father and father-in-law to the owners, friendly welcomer of visitors and one of those people who restore your faith in the goodness of humankind. Turn up here without cooking equipment and he'll even pop whatever you've got into the microwave for you.

While Bude will always be the number one attraction for campers here, both Clovelly (14 miles) and Hartland Point (15 miles) are within striking distance, and a pleasant half-hour walk across fields and down a lane will take you to Sandymouth with its eponymous beaches of golden sand.

4 Little Wenfork

Rezare
Launceston
Cornwall
PL15 9NU

Mike and Sam Wing
01579 370755
info@littlewenfork.co.uk
www.littlewenfork.co.uk
Landranger: 201 (SX 354 774)

THE BASICS
Size: ½ acre.
Pitches: 5 (2 hard standing). Max. 12 people on site.
Terrain: Slightly sloping.
Shelter: Hedge shelters from east and west.
View: Kit Hill.
Waterside: No.
Electric hook-ups: No.
Noise/Light/Olfactory pollution: No.

THE FACILITIES
Loos: 1U. **Showers**: 1U (free).
Other facilities: Outdoor washing-up area, freezer block freezing service, CDP, free-range eggs for sale.
Stuff for children: Animals to pet.
Recycling: Everything.

THE RULES
Dogs: On leads.
Fires: Platform for fire at top of field and oil drums available to use as braziers.
Other: Close the gate to keep cows out.

PUB LIFE
The Springer Spaniel (free house), Treburley (½ mile) – 18th-century pub serving locally sourced food, some of which is from its own organic farm; open Sun–Thur 12–3pm & 6–11pm, Fri & Sat till midnight; food served 12–1:45pm & 6:30–8:45pm 7D; 01579 370424; www.thespringerspaniel.org.uk.

SHOP
Stoke Climsland PO (2½ miles) – small but packed to the rafters with supplies; open Mon–Fri 7am–6pm, Sat till 12:30pm, Sun 8–11am; 01579 370201.

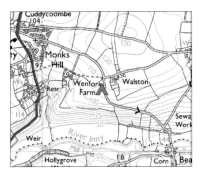

THERE AND AWAY
Train station: Gunnislake (13 miles) – Gunnislake to Plymouth line. Take bus no. 79 to Callington, then hop on the 576, which stops at the Springer Spaniel pub.

OUT AND ABOUT
Cotehele (9 miles) – magnificent and reputedly haunted Tudor house in large grounds; visit can be combined with a boat trip (see below); adult £8.30, child £4.15, family £20.75; open mid March to October, Sat–Thur 11am–4:30pm; 01579 351346; NT site.
Calstock ferry – take a trip between Calstock (9 miles) and Cotehele (9 miles) along the Tamar river, one of the loveliest county boundaries in Britain; sailings timetable depends on tide: check website for details; adult £4 return, child £3; 01822 833331; www.calstockferry.co.uk.

open	April to October
tiny campsites' rating	★ ★
friendliness	☺ ☺ ☺
cost	BP ££, Couple ££, Family ££

There's a mystery surrounding Little Wenfork. This thin half-acre slip of land has divided two neighbouring farms for hundreds of years, but no one is quite sure why it's there when all the fields around it are, well, proper field size. A further layer of intrigue is supplied by the deeds, which show that in the 1800s the cigar-shaped plot was lost (and thus also won) in a bet. With regard to the how and the why of the wager, however, the documents remain stubbornly silent.

Today's owners are unlikely to hand the field over to you on the turn of a single card but, as consolation, you can enjoy a cracking view of Kit Hill and parts of the Tamar Valley, an Area of Outstanding Natural Beauty. In case you missed it in the news, the hill was given to the villagers of Callington by Prince Charles on the birth of his son William. The area is now a country park open to the public and, on a clear day, views of both the north and the south coasts of Cornwall can be seen from the top.

A small allotment on the campsite is home to ducks, chickens and some Gloucestershire Old Spots pigs who love having their heads scratched. Children (and adults too) are at liberty to test for themselves just how great this love is. Most of the time, however, visitors are content to lie back and enjoy the wide Cornish skies that Little Wenfork, perched up on a hill, seems very close to indeed.

Clifford Bridge
Drewsteignton
Devon
EX6 6QB

Mr and Mrs JR Guillebaud
01647 24331
jrguillebaud@gmail.com
Landranger: 191 (SX 780 900)

THE BASICS
Size: ⅕ acre field & 4 small garden pitches.
Pitches: 8 (0 hard standing).
Terrain: Mainly flat.
Shelter: On all sides.
View: No.
Waterside: No.
Electric hook-ups: Potentially 1 (they've got an extension lead).
Noise/Light/Olfactory pollution: No.

THE FACILITIES
Loos: 1U. **Showers**: 1U (free).
Other facilities: No.
Stuff for children: Trampoline, swing, pony-sitting by arrangement.
Recycling: Glass, tins, plastic milk bottles.

THE RULES
Dogs: If well behaved.
Fires: Yes, in the field, but only if there hasn't been a drought (please bring/ scavenge for your own wood); BBQs off ground. **Other**: No.

PUB LIFE
Royal Oak (free house), Dunsford (2½ miles) – a family-run country pub with a walled courtyard; open in summer Mon 7–9pm, Tue–Sat 12–2:30pm & 6:30–11pm, Sun 7–11pm; food served Sun–Mon 7–8pm, Tue–Sat 12–2pm & 7–9pm; 01647 252256; www.royaloakd.com. Or else you can opt to walk or cycle westwards along the River Teign to the **Fingle Bridge Inn** (free house), Drewsteignton (3 miles) – beer garden right on the river; open in summer Mon–Sat 11am–10pm, Sun till 6pm; food served Mon–Sat 12–4:30pm & 6–9pm, Sun

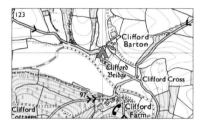

12–3pm (daily cream teas till 5pm); 01647 281287; www.finglebridgeinn.com.

SHOP
Dunsford PO (2½ miles) – very basic supplies and newspapers; open Mon–Fri 8:30am–5pm (closed 1–2pm daily and Wed afternoons), Sat 9am–1pm; 01647 252330. There's also a **Co-op** in Moretonhampstead (3 miles) and **Chequers Store** in Cheriton Bishop (3 miles).

THERE AND AWAY
Train station: Yeoford (6¾ miles) – Exeter to Barnstaple line (aka the Tarka Line). Take a taxi from here as there's no onward bus.

OUT AND ABOUT
Castle Drogo (4½ miles) – the last castle built in England (and by Edwin Lutyens to boot); adult £7.45, child £3.72, family £18.63; open daily mid March to October 11am–5pm (see website for rest of year); 01647 433306; NT site.
Finch Foundry, Sticklepath (9¾ miles) – England's last working water-powered forge; adult £4.20, child £2.10; open mid March to October Wed–Mon 11am–5pm; 01837 840046; NT site.

open	All year
tiny campsites' rating	★ ★
friendliness	☺☺☺
cost	BP ££, Couple ££, Family ££

If the ultimate expression of tiny camping is to pitch your tent in someone's back garden, then Sweet Meadows, on the north-eastern edge of Dartmoor, is it. Sliding past the corner of the house, you'll have to brush aside flowers competing for space in order to make it on to the back lawn with its elegant cast-iron table and chairs.

There is a very small field for camping on the other side of a hedge but, when booking, nab a place in the garden and ask for the pitch nearest the house. Of the four lovely spaces there, this one – surrounded on three sides by flowerbeds (often blissfully overgrown) and shaded by an apple tree – is so perfect you'll be hugging yourself with joy when you reach it.

Beyond, an arch in the hedge reveals a tree-swing and the wilder regions of the garden where less clearly defined pitches take on an altogether more rustic feel. The small field looks on to a paddock where the owners graze their Isle of Rum ponies. On request, the pony known as Flossie (officially Donna of Carrick), can be saddled for kids to sit on.

Meanwhile, the shower/loo is a homely bathroom in the house, with access from the garden.

Nature-lovers need only sit by their tent and wait. The garden is visited by owls, three sorts of woodpecker, buzzards, sparrowhawks and hobbies, as well as fallow, roe and red deer. Just beyond the hedge, the woods of the Teign Valley are renowned for their daffodils and early-purple and spotted orchids, while just half a mile away there's a nature reserve at Steps Bridge.

6 Millslade

Millslade Country House
Brendon
Lynton
Devon
EX35 6PS

Keith and Carol Cobb
01598 741322
keithcarol@millslade.wanadoo.co.uk
www.millslade.co.uk
OS Landranger: 180 (SS 765 481)

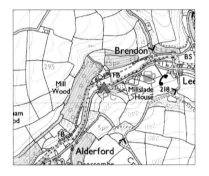

THE BASICS
Size: ⅓ acre.
Pitches: 20 (0 hard standing).
Terrain: Flat.
Shelter: All round – mainly beech and sycamore trees.
View: No.
Waterside: Yes, the East Lyn river.
Electric hook-ups: No.
Noise/Light/Olfactory pollution: The gurgle of the East Lyn.

THE FACILITIES
Loos: 2M 3W. **Showers**: No.
Other facilities: Cold water washbasins.
Stuff for children: Swing above river, adventure playground in next field.
Recycling: Everything.

THE RULES
Dogs: Under control.
Fires: Open fires allowed (please bring your own wood); BBQs off grass or in the fire pit. **Other**: No.

PUB LIFE
Stag Hunters Hotel (free house), Brendon (200 metres) – the oldest section of the pub was Millslade Abbey's chapel before Henry VIII dissolved it. The food comes recommended and they also sell a £1 book of local walks; open 12–3pm & 6–11:30pm 7D; food served Mon–Sat 12–2:30pm & 6–9pm, Sun 12–2pm & 7–9pm; 01598 741222; www.staghunters.com.

SHOP
Costcutter, Lynton (4 miles) – large convenience store and off licence; open 7am–9pm 7D; 01598 753438.

THERE AND AWAY
Train station: Barnstaple (22 miles) – Barnstaple to Exeter line (aka the Tarka Line). Bus no. 310 runs between Barnstaple and Lynton.

OUT AND ABOUT
Lynmouth (3½ miles) – wonderful (if rather touristy) harbour on the precipitous River Lyn and scene of notorious floods in 1952; 0845 6603232; www.lynton-lynmouth-tourism.co.uk.
Lynton & Barnstaple Railway (6¾ miles) – despite its name, the L&BR actually runs for just a mile between Woody Bay station and Killington Lane, but its tiny steam engines have got 'happy summertime memory' written all over them (though not literally, of course); adult return £6, U14 £3; open daily in summer, for timetable see website; 01598 763487; www.lynton-rail.co.uk.

DEVON

open	March to October
tiny campsites' rating	✴ ✴
friendliness	☺
cost	BP £, Couple ££, Family ££££

Whether you come by car, bike or on foot, the most satisfying way to approach Brendon is by hauling yourself up on to Exmoor from Lynmouth. After scaling Countisbury Hill, an unrelenting and often quite steep climb, and catching the extraordinary view at the top (while being blown about by the inevitable gales), the descent into cosy Brendon is an unalloyed joy. The shelter this little valley settlement affords gives you the feeling of having snuggled into a particularly comfortable bed.

Breezing over the bridge that crosses the East Lyn river, once Brendon's main street, you'll find Millslade a few hundred metres to the west, marking the edge of a village that squeezes itself into the valley bottom like a line of toothpaste. This is no ordinary valley either, but is known as Hidden Valley or Lorna Doone Valley, according to taste. Malmsmead, where much of RD Blackmore's book was set, is just a couple of miles along the river.

The campsite, in common with the village, stretches itself along the East Lyn. Hedges and trees afford protection, loos come courtesy of a Portakabin, but drinking water must be collected from Millslade House, about 100 metres away.

In the local inn, the Stag Hunters Hotel, Doone-esque conversations can still be heard. Ask them to tell you about the rogue who, adding to his list of alleged petty crimes (and progeny in every village) is suspected of having killed the largest stag in the area. It's a different world all right.

West Bradley
Glastonbury
Somerset
BA6 8LU

David and Lene Cotton
01458 850431
info@bridgefarmcaravansite.co.uk
www.bridgefarmcaravansite.co.uk
Landranger: 183 (ST 552 363)

THE BASICS
Size: ⅗ acre.
Pitches: 12 (0 hard standing). Max. 5 motorhomes per night.
Terrain: Flat.
Shelter: From all sides but north.
View: Glastonbury Tor.
Waterside: No.
Electric hook-ups: 6.
Noise/Light/Olfactory pollution: No.

THE FACILITIES
Loos: 1M 1W. **Showers**: 1U (free).
Other facilities: Washing-up area, plug for phone chargers, CDP, freezer for ice blocks.
Stuff for children: Milking time can be watched on request.
Recycling: Everything.

THE RULES
Dogs: On leads. **Fires**: No open fires; BBQs off grass. **Other**: No.

PUB LIFE
The Lion (Punch Taverns), West Pennard (2 miles) – a friendly country pub that plays host to morris dancers on occasion; open 12–3pm & 6–11pm 7D (Sun till 10:30pm); food served 12–2:15pm & 6–9:15pm; 01458 832941.

SHOP
Baltonsborough PO (1¾ miles) – basic supplies and a small off licence; open Mon–Fri 8:30am–1pm & 2–6pm, Sat 8:30am–1pm, Sun till 11am; 01458 850249.

THERE AND AWAY
Train station: Castle Cary (8 miles) – London to Exeter line. Nippy Bus Ltd

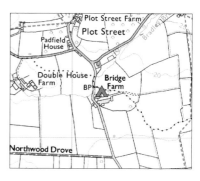

(www.nippybus.co.uk) runs bus no. 667 between Castle Cary and West Bradley.

OUT AND ABOUT
Glastonbury Abbey (4½ miles) – set in 36 acres of parkland, this reputed burial place of King Arthur was also Britain's largest abbey; adult £5, child £3, U5 free; open daily June to August 9am–6pm, rest of year open daily at varying times; 01458 832267; www.glastonburyabbey.com.
Glastonbury Tor (3 miles) – the focal point for more myths and legends than you can shake an enchanted stick at, plus an astonishing view from the top; free; always open; 01934 844518; NT site.
Wookey Hole Caves, nr Wells (11 miles) – home not only to huge piles of maturing Cheddar cheese but a whole 'Wookey Hole Experience' that boasts its very own witch (a former estate agent); adult £15, child (3–14 years old) £10, family £45; open daily April to October 10am–5pm (last tour), November to March 10am–4pm; 01749 672243; www.wookey.co.uk.

open	Easter to Halloween
tiny campsites' rating	★ ★
friendliness	☺☺
cost	BP ££, Couple ££, Family ££

Glastonbury Tor, with the sun setting behind its simple church tower, makes for one of the great iconic views of England. It's also home to the King of the Fairies, Gwyn ap Nudd, so it's nice to know that such a regal spot can be enjoyed from an unfussy field on a farm on the Somerset Levels.

Of course, had you come here many hundreds of years ago, you could have reached the Tor by boat, possibly sailing right over Bridge Farm in the process. Legend has it that the teenage Jesus visited here with Joseph of Arimathea, an unlikely event that inspired William Blake to pen 'Jerusalem'.

The campsite on the 600-acre Bridge Farm is a simple square, bordered on three sides by hedges. Meanwhile, the generously sized loos and shower are a short walk away through an adjoining field.

The quiet, flat roads around the farm are perfect for novice cyclists or, indeed, experienced cyclists who want to take it easy. There's a National Byway Loop (www.thenationalbyway.org) very close by that uses minor roads to form a circuit taking in Glastonbury and Wells (turn left out of the farm then left again to join it). Alternatively, you could make up your own local route, perhaps touring the many vineyards and cider orchards that strew the area.

Glastonbury itself is a relatively level and almost car-free five miles away on back roads, should you wish to experience a gong bath or a Tibetan eye-reading, or merely need to take your crystals in for a service.

Spyway
Askerswell
Bridport
Dorset
DT2 9EP

Tim Wilkes
01308 485250
tim.wilkes@btconnect.com
www.spyway-inn.com
OS Landranger: 194 (SY 528 932)

THE BASICS
Size: 1/20 acre.
Pitches: 4 (0 hard standing).
Terrain: Mainly flat.
Shelter: All sides.
View: Askerswell church and Iron Age fort.
Waterside: Just about.
Electric hook-ups: No.
Noise/Light/Olfactory pollution: Some light from pub; the enticing smells of breakfast in the morning.

THE FACILITIES
Loos: 1U. **Showers:** 1U (free).
Other facilities: No.
Stuff for children: No.
Recycling: No.

THE RULES
Dogs: No. **Fires:** No open fires; BBQs off grass. **Other:** No.

PUB LIFE
Spyway Inn (free house), a peg's throw from the tent; open 12–3pm & 6pm 'until we close' 7D; food served 12–3pm & 6:30–9(ish)pm 7D.

SHOP
Co-op, Bridport (4½ miles) – small supermarket; open Mon–Sat 8am–10pm, Sun 10am–4pm; 01308 421541. The Spyway can also supply campers with basic bits and pieces.

THERE AND AWAY
Train station: Maiden Newton (6 miles) – Bristol to Weymouth (aka Heart of Wessex) line. No direct bus service from Maiden Newton to Spyway, so hop in a taxi.

OUT AND ABOUT
Chesil Beach (9 miles) – an extraordinary 18-mile shingle beach on Dorset's Jurassic Coast that stretches from the Isle of Portland to West Bay, consisting, apparently, of 180 billion pebbles, though it's unclear who counted them, or why; www.chesilbeach.org.
Iron Age hill forts – Chilcombe and Eggardon are right on your doorstep, but the immensely impressive Maiden Castle is only 10 miles east – it's the largest Iron Age hill fort in Britain (and possibly in Europe) and was occupied for 4,000 years before being taken by the Romans in AD 43; free; always open; www.english-heritage.org.uk.

open	All year
tiny campsites' rating	★ ★ ★
friendliness	☺
cost	BP £, Couple ££, Family ££££

Is this the smallest pub campsite in Britain? At just 15 strides one way and 14 the other, if you're going to bring a cat along with you to swing, you'd better make sure it's a small one. Happily, the novelty of this site's compactness is by no means its only charm. There are its two Christmas trees, for a start. A flowerbed sporting fluffy, pink hemp agrimony, while an appropriately miniscule stream tinkles along the foot of the lawn.

The 18th-century pub whose garden the campsite adjoins is on the miniature side too – just a bijou bar and a room for meals. Since the food served there has something of a reputation in these parts (and has gained the Spyway an inclusion in the *Good Pub Guide*), it's a good idea to book your table, especially towards the end of the week. It's worthwhile booking your pitch too, since it really doesn't take much for the campsite to become full.

The view, however, is anything but small. The tower of Askerswell Church is dwarfed by Chilcombe Hill beyond, topped by its Iron Age hill fort. The walk from the pub through fields to Eggardon Hill (which also has an Iron Age hill fort: it makes you wonder if Iron Age men did anything other than building) and back makes an excellent pre-prandial appetite-whetter.

Students of the history of tax evasion will be excited to learn that the inn was once owned by notorious smuggler Isaac Gulliver and is reputedly haunted (though not necessarily by him).

South-Central England

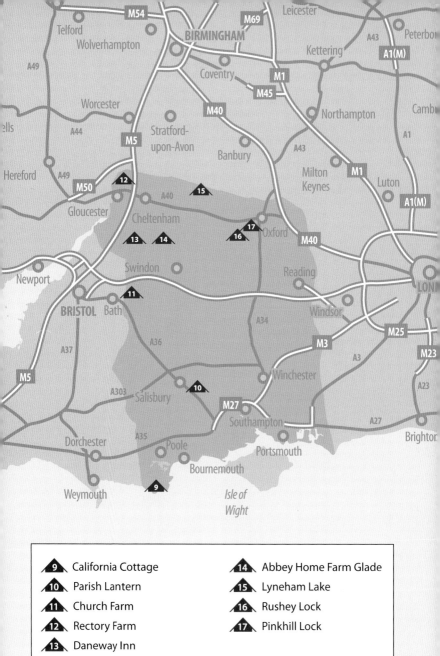

9 California Cottage	14 Abbey Home Farm Glade
10 Parish Lantern	15 Lyneham Lake
11 Church Farm	16 Rushey Lock
12 Rectory Farm	17 Pinkhill Lock
13 Daneway Inn	

9 California Cottage

Priests Way
Swanage
Dorset BH19 2RS
(Don't use postcode
in GPS – see website
for directions.)

Karen Delahay
01929 425049
queries@californiabarn.co.uk
www.californiabarn.co.uk
Landranger: 195 (SZ 019 777)

THE BASICS
Size: ²/₅ acre.
Pitches: 15 (0 hard standing).
Terrain: Gently sloping.
Shelter: Trees to south-west.
View: Surrounding fields.
Waterside: No.
Electric hook-ups: No.
Noise/Light/Olfactory pollution: 2 mysterious bright lights about a mile away; some steam-train hoots.

THE FACILITIES
Loos: 2M 2W. **Showers**: No.
Other facilities: Outdoor washing-up area.
Stuff for children: No.
Recycling: Bottles, cans, plastic.

THE RULES
Dogs: If well behaved.
Fires: Designated fire pit by loo block; BBQs off grass. **Other**: No.

PUB LIFE
Black Swan Inn (free house), High Street, Swanage (1 mile) – good food and frequent live folk and blues music; open Mon–Fri 5:30–11pm, w/es 12–2:30pm & 5:30–11pm; food served Mon–Fri 6–8:45pm, w/es 12–2pm & 6–8:45pm; 01929 423846; www.blackswanswanage. co.uk. Or if you fancy a walk across the fields, try the **Square and Compass** (free house), Worth Matravers (4 miles) – pub with its own fossil museum and jazz festival, and where the only food served is pies and pasties (veg ones available too); open 12–11pm 7D during summer; pasties served all day; 01929 439229; www.squareandcompasspub.co.uk.

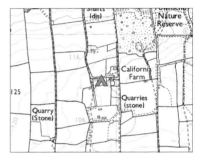

SHOP
Costcutter, Herston (1 mile) – mini supermarket, newspapers, off licence; 7am–8pm 7D; 01929 422549.

THERE AND AWAY
Train station: Wareham (10 miles) – London to Weymouth line. Wiltshire and Dorset bus company (www. wdbus.co.uk) runs an hourly no. 40 service from Wareham station to Swanage.

OUT AND ABOUT
Swanage Railway (1¼ miles) – 6 miles of heritage railway over the beautiful Purbeck Hills via Corfe Castle; Swanage to Norden adult return £9, child £7, family £26 – discounted tickets available; 01929 425800; www.swanagerailway.co.uk.
Studland Beach and Nature Reserve (5 miles) – 3 miles of sandy beaches and a haven for rare birds and wildlife; free; always open; 01929 450259; NT site.

A

open	Variable: ring for details
tiny campsites' rating	★★
friendliness	☺☺
cost	BP ££, Couple ££, Family £££

Among the many charms of California Cottage are the somewhat convoluted directions for getting there. These take you through a munchkinland mobile-home park, over a hill (on a rough track rather than a yellow brick road) and through various gates, until suddenly you've arrived in a small field by a quarry just two fields from the sea.

The sense of it being your own private plot of land is accentuated by the lack of any adjacent buildings and the thoroughgoing rusticity of the facilities. A washing-up sink stands in the open air next to a standpipe, while a muddy path, charmingly lit at night by a line of solar lights, leads down into a copse that hides the toilet block. The only light in the loos comes from a tiny LED fixture, so do remember to take a torch along. This is not a site for those who when they say the word 'camping' are actually thinking the word 'glamping'.

Next to the block is a fire pit surrounded by an eclectic assortment of chairs and benches, while a pile of crates stands ready to be broken up into fuel for the flames.

Walk out the other side of the copse, and in two minutes you'll find yourself in Durlston Country Park (www.durlston.co.uk), a wonderland of wild flowers, tumbling ravines and ragged cliffs, along which runs the South West Coast Path (www.southwestcoastpath.com). The cliffs are also home to the Tilly Whim Caves, a whale-watching hide and a café.

10 **Parish Lantern**

Romsey Road
Whiteparish
Salisbury
Wiltshire
SP5 2SA

Paul and Lorraine Cooper
01794 884392
paul@theparishlantern.co.uk
www.theparishlantern.co.uk
OS Landranger: 184 (SU 248 237)

THE BASICS
Size: ⅖ acre.
Pitches: 5 (1 hard standing).
Terrain: Flat.
Shelter: On all sides except to south-east.
View: Across a field.
Waterside: No.
Electric hook-ups: No.
Noise/Light/Olfactory pollution: Leave-taking at pub.

THE FACILITIES
Loos: 1M 2W. **Showers**: No.
Other facilities: No.
Stuff for children: Play area including slide, swings and 2 trampolines.
Recycling: No.

THE RULES
Dogs: On leads.
Fires: No open fires; BBQs off grass.
Other: No.

PUB LIFE
Parish Lantern (free house), 20 metres; open Mon–Thur 11:30am–2:30pm & 5–11pm, Fri–Sun 11:30am–11pm; food served 12–2pm & 6:30–9pm 7D.

SHOP
Whiteparish PO (¼ mile) – basics plus a small off licence; open Mon–Fri 7:30am–5:30pm, Sat 8:30am–5pm, Sun till midday; 01794 884221.

THERE AND AWAY
Train station: Dean (2½ miles) – Salisbury to Southampton line. No direct bus service onward to Whiteparish, so hop into a taxi.

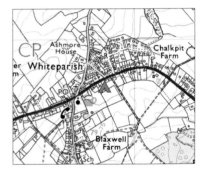

OUT AND ABOUT
The New Forest (½ mile) – covering an area of about 220 square miles, there's as much walking, cycling and wildlife-watching on offer to fulfil the heart's desire of any man, woman or child; www.new-forest-national-park.com.
Stonehenge, nr Amesbury (18 miles) – where the dewdrops cry and the cats miaow, and huge 5,000-year-old stones from the Preseli Mountains continue to puzzle all comers; adult £6.60, child (5–15 years-old) £3.30; open daily June to August 9am–7pm (opening hours vary for the rest of the year); 01980 622833; www.english-heritage.org.uk.
Salisbury (9 miles) – a city with an inspiring medieval cathedral (01722 555120; www.salisburycathedral.org.uk), an enticing little museum (01722 332151; tinyurl.com/ykmdcos), a great number of fairs and festivals, and much else besides.

open	All year
tiny campsites' rating	★
friendliness	☺☺
cost	BP £, Couple £, Family £

Some pubs have either a campsite or a beer garden around the back. Others have both a campsite and a beer garden. But rare indeed is the pub whose beer garden *is* the campsite. Such is the case at the Parish Lantern, where the frontier between camping and sitting around drinking has been bravely dispensed with, ushering in a new era in which picnic tables and guy ropes may live in harmony. This radical mix is further enriched throughout the small field by the sprinkling of children's playthings including four swings, two trampolines and some sort of maniacal infant-eating tree that doubles as a slide. Just to top it off, there are chickens in a large run, some of whom have floppy feather-covered feet and no doubt go by the name of New Forest Whites, or Dandy Highwaymen or similar.

The view from the campsite, though not spectacular, is one that soothes the soul: an open vista across a field to woods and low hills beyond. Closer to home, the loos are available only during the pub's open hours, so it's advisable to time your visits wisely.

The village of Whiteparish is just outside the northern edge of the New Forest, Henry VIII's former hunting ground and now the des res of wild ponies, five different sorts of deer, three types of snake (adder, smooth and grass), newts, frogs, toads and Britain's rarest reptile, the sand lizard. To maximise your chances of spotting some of the forest's littler inhabitants, hit the one-and-a-half-mile reptile trail that loops out from the New Forest Reptile Centre (tinyurl.com/yzanmwe).

11 Church Farm

Monkton Farleigh
Bradford-on-Avon
Wiltshire
BA15 2QJ

Chris and Di Tucker

01225 858583 & 07803 966798

reservations@churchfarmmonktonfarleigh.co.uk

www.churchfarmmonktonfarleigh.co.uk

OS Landranger: 173 (ST 808 651)

THE BASICS
Size: ⁴/₅ acre.
Pitches: 10 (0 hard standing)
Terrain: Mainly sloping.
Shelter: A long hedge.
View: Westbury White Horse,
Salisbury Plain.
Waterside: Pond at bottom of field.
Electric hook-ups: No.
Noise/Light/Olfactory pollution:
Occasional neighs and stomping of horses'
hoofs; RAF airfield nearby.

THE FACILITIES
Loos: 1M 1W. **Showers**: 1M 1W (free).
Other facilities: Outdoor heated-pool,
washing-up area, microwave, kettle.
Stuff for children: Trampoline, tree swing,
slide.
Recycling: Glass.

THE RULES
Dogs: Under control.
Fires: Open fires; BBQs off grass.
Other: Don't feed the horses.

PUB LIFE
King's Arms (Punch Taverns), Monkton
Farleigh (¼ mile) – a former manor house
now decked out with classy cushioned
pews, big sofas, subdued lighting and
soothing Röyksopp sounds; open Mon–Fri
12–3pm & 6–11pm, Sat 12–11pm, Sun
till 9pm; food served Mon–Fri 12–3pm &
6–10pm, Sat 12–10pm, Sun till 9pm; 01225
858705; www.kingsarms-bath.co.uk.

SHOP
Monkton Farleigh PO (¼ mile) – small but
comprehensive shop with a range from

super-cheap Euroshopper food to less
cheap organics; open Mon–Fri 9am–1pm &
2–5:30pm, Sat 9am–1pm; 01225 858258.

THERE AND AWAY
Train station: Bradford-on-Avon (4¼ miles)
– Bath to Trowbridge line. Libra Travel's bus
no. 96 travels occasionally from Bradford-
on-Avon to Monkton Farleigh.

OUT AND ABOUT
Bath (5 miles) – founded by the Romans
as *Aquae Sulis* and since established as a
tourist magnet by John Wood, architect of
the city's famous Circus (setting for many
a period drama), and Jane Austen, author
and astute commentator on social mores;
www.visitbath.co.uk.
Bradford-on-Avon (4 miles) – lovely small
town, also established by those busy
Romans, boasting a Saxon church that was
hidden for hundreds of years and oodles of
venerable Bath Stone buildings;
01225 865797 (tourist information centre);
www.bradfordonavon.co.uk.

open	All year
tiny campsites' rating	★ ★
friendliness	☺ ☺
cost	BP ££, Couple ££, Family ££

The village of Monkton Farleigh, if not necessarily posh, certainly strikes the casual visitor as well-heeled. The pub injects a dose of cosmopolitan cool into this quiet chunk of countryside, the village shop is piled high with organic produce and the cars standing outside the neat stone cottages are shiny and German. Even Church Farm is not a farm in the usual arable/livestock sense, but is populated exclusively by horses who roam its 50 acres looking for trouble – but rarely finding it.

It's a pleasure, then, to discover that there are no airs or graces about the campsite itself. A simple field slopes down a hillside and enjoys a phenomenal vista of the countryside below. In the distance, the Westbury White Horse is caught in perpetual inertia contemplating the Bratton Downs, while to its left rises Caen Hill with Salisbury Plain beyond.

The loos and showers are in a large barn that also stables horses – you pass them on your way in and out – which is unusual for a campsite to say the least. However, even that is trumped by the outdoor heated pool, which is available to campers from lunchtime until 3pm each day in summertime for £3 a pop.

Walkers will relish the jaunt up a hill called Farleigh Rise, which takes off from the north end of the village, while cyclists can drop down to the Kennet and Avon Canal to enjoy a cycle path that stretches from Bath all the way to Reading.

Lawn Road
Ashleworth
Gloucestershire
GL19 4JL

Mr and Mrs MG Houldey
01452 700664
angela_houldey@o2.co.uk
www.rectoryfarm-caravanandcamping.com
Landranger: 162 (SO 802 262)

THE BASICS
Size: ²/₅ acre.
Pitches: Variable (0 hard standing).
Terrain: Flat.
Shelter: Yes.
View: Adjoining fields replete with sheep.
Waterside: No.
Electric hook-ups: No.
Noise/Light/Olfactory pollution: Some traffic noise from A417 across the fields.

THE FACILITIES
Loos: No. **Showers**: No.
Other facilities: CDP.
Stuff for children: Trampoline.
Recycling: Everything.

THE RULES
Dogs: On leads (there are sheep about).
Fires: No open fires; BBQs off grass.
Other: No.

PUB LIFE
Watersmeet Country Inn (free house), Hartpury (¼ miles by footpath) – a hotel bar with a log fire, its own 10-acre wood and 3 lakes; open 8:30am–'midnight-ish'; breakfast served 8:30–9:30am 7D; food served Mon–Fri 12–2:30pm & 6:30–9pm, Sat 12–9pm, Sun till 8pm; 01452 700358; www.watersmeetcountryinn.co.uk.

SHOP
Ashleworth PO (¾ mile) – basics and off licence; open Mon–Fri 7:30am–1pm & 2–5:30pm, Sat 9am–4pm; 01452 700215.
St George's Bakery, Corse (½ mile) – fresh bread and other baked goodies; open Mon–Fri 8:30am–5pm, Sat 9am–noon; 01452 700234.

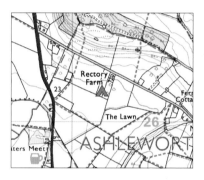

THERE AND AWAY
Train station: Gloucester (7¼ miles) – London to Gloucester line. Regular buses run between Gloucester and Tewkesbury, stopping near the site.

OUT AND ABOUT
Severn Way, Haw Bridge (3¾ miles) – the longest river walk in Britain, a full 210 miles from Plynlimon in Wales to the Bristol Channel; www.severnway.com.
Gloucester (7 miles) – a compact city packed with delights from the cathedral to the Victorian docks; 01452 396572 (tourist information office); www.gloucester.gov.uk/tourism.
Malvern Hills (8 miles) – a glorious 8-mile ridge that resembles a scale model of a 'proper' mountain range like Snowdonia, the Cairngorms or indeed the Himalayas (George Mallory practised here for his ill-fated assault on Everest); 01684 892002; www.malvernhills.org.uk.

open	Easter to October
tiny campsites' rating	★
friendliness	☺☺
cost	BP ££, Couple ££, Family ££

GLOUCESTERSHIRE

If you head west out of the Cotswolds and stop before you reach the Wye Valley you'll find yourself in an area of Gloucestershire that remains largely uncharted. Here the River Severn slides calmly through flat fields in which simple labourers toil away with mattock and scythe until their daily bread is won. Or so it once was, probably. In the midst of what is now a thoroughly modern rural landscape sits Rectory Farm, a modest 60-acre sheep farm sitting just outside the quiet village of Ashleworth.

The camping area has the feel of a back garden crossed with a farm site. On one side there are flowerbeds spread out around the owners' house, while on the other a flock of sheep mosey about mulling over which juicy blade of grass to go for next. A static caravan is tucked away to one side, while a trampoline provides children with endless hours of bouncy giggles. There are no other facilities here as yet, but the owners do have plans to install a loo and shower in a barn sometime soon.

If you visit around August Bank Holiday you'll be able to experience the maelstrom of creative invention that is the local scarecrow competition, held annually at Ashleworth, a mile to the east. In 2009, Douglas Bader and a singing Loch Ness Monster were pipped by a Cyclops. Meanwhile, just two fields away, there's a pub (actually a hotel bar, but that does mean it serves food from 8:30am, which is definitely a bonus if you're a few cornflakes short of a breakfast).

13 Daneway Inn

Daneway
Sapperton
Cirencester
Gloucestershire
GL7 6LN

Richard and Elizabeth Goodfellow
01285 760297
info@thedaneway.com
www.thedaneway.com
OS Landranger: 163 (SO 939 033)

THE BASICS
Size: ³/₅ acre.
Pitches: 5 (0 hard standing).
Terrain: Some flat, some slopey, some bumpy.
Shelter: All sides.
View: A little way up the Dane Valley.
Waterside: Disused Thames and Severn Canal.
Electric hook-ups: No.
Noise/Light/Olfactory pollution: No.

THE FACILITIES
Loos: 1M 1W (in pub). **Showers**: No.
Other facilities: No.
Stuff for children: No.
Recycling: Glass, paper, plastics.

THE RULES
Dogs: If well behaved (livestock next door).
Fires: No open fires; BBQs off grass.
Other: No large groups.

PUB LIFE
Daneway Inn (on site) – a cosy, friendly, rustic pub; quiz night Weds, open-mic music night Tues; open Mon–Fri 11am–2:30pm & 6:30–11pm (closed Mon eves), w/es 11am–11pm; food served 12–2pm & 7–9pm 7D (except Mon eves).

SHOP
Oakridge Lynch PO (2½ miles) – essentials, newspapers, a small off licence and an internet café; open Mon–Fri 8am–7pm, Sat 8am–2pm, Sun till 1pm; 01285 760239.

THERE AND AWAY
Train station: Kemble (6 miles) – London to Gloucester line. The Cotswold Green

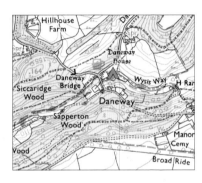

bus no. 54 runs from Stroud train station to Sapperton, a 10-minute walk from the site.

OUT AND ABOUT
Thames Path (4½ miles) – the source of the Thames is but a 90-minute ramble away, making the Daneway a great spot to start or finish a jaunty trek along the mighty river; 01865 810224; www.nationaltrail.co.uk/Thamespath.
Cotswold Water Park (9½ miles) – 140 lakes in 40 square miles of parkland, with a huge range of activities to try out on land or water from paintballing to wakeboarding; 01793 752413; www.waterpark.org. (Also accessible from Abbey Home Farm Glade, p50.)

open	March to end September
tiny campsites' rating	✷ ✷
friendliness	☺☺☺
cost	BP £, Couple ££, Family ££

GLOUCESTERSHIRE

Richard, the landlord of the Daneway Inn, is apt to refer to the experience of spending the night at his campsite as 'camping *sauvage*', and indeed it does take pub camping off to a very unusual place. Rather than a neat and trim level site, the field next to the Daneway careers off around a corner into a wood and slopes down to a long-disused canal, which, in heavy rain is liable to flood. Fortunately, there's plenty of space high enough above the canal (that for all the world looks like a mere stream nowadays) for this not to pose too much of a problem. The grass is also left long enough for the place to look refreshingly untamed, and the picture is completed by the goodly number of wild plants that grow up through it.

The inn itself is one of those perfect off-the-beaten-track pubs that other people brag about discovering, but which seldom seem to crop up on one's own travels. Originally built as three cottages in 1784 for navvies digging the canal, it serves real ale, has quiz and open-mic music nights ('everyone welcome'), and boasts an astonishing floor-to-ceiling carved fireplace rescued from what must have been a huge house.

As for the conveniences, the men get a better deal, theirs being accessible 24 hours a day. The ladies' loo, being inside the pub, is available only during opening hours. There are a lot of trees to wander behind, however. This is, after all, camping *sauvage*.

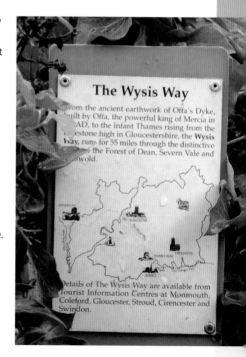

The Wysis Way

...om the ancient earthwork of Offa's Dyke, ...uilt by Offa, the powerful king of Mercia in ...AD, to the infant Thames rising from the ...estone high in Gloucestershire, the **Wysis** Way, runs for 55 miles through the distinctive ...the Forest of Dean, Severn Vale and ...swold.

Details of The Wysis Way are available from Tourist Information Centres at Monmouth, Coleford, Gloucester, Stroud, Cirencester and Swindon.

Abbey Home Farm Glade

The Organic Farm Shop
Burford Road
Cirencester
Gloucestershire
GL7 5HF

Will and Hilary Chester-Master

01285 640441

hilary@theorganicfarmshop.co.uk

www.theorganicfarmshop.co.uk

Landranger: 163 (SP 042 037)

THE BASICS
Size: 2 little clearings x ¹⁄₄₀ acre.
Pitches: 4 (0 hard standing). Max. 8 people per night.
Terrain: Flat.
Shelter: Yes.
View: No.
Waterside: No.
Electric hook-ups: No.
Noise/Light/Olfactory pollution: No.

THE FACILITIES
Loos (compost): 1U. **Showers**: No.
Other facilities: No.
Stuff for children: Woodland to explore; colourful totem poles to run around.
Recycling: Everything.

THE RULES
Dogs: No. **Fires**: Open fires in tractor wheel (firewood £5/bag).
Other: 2-night minimum stay; take all non-recyclable rubbish away with you.

PUB LIFE
The Village Pub (free house), Barnsley (3½ miles) – yes, the pub is actually called that; it's very pretty and a swish gastro affair to boot (and yes, it's a different Barnsley); open Mon–Fri 11am–3:30pm & 6–11pm, Sat 11am–11pm, Sun 12–10:30pm; lunch served Mon–Fri 12–2:30pm, w/es till 3pm, dinner served Sun–Thur 7–9:30pm, Fri–Sat till 10pm; 01285 740421; www.thevillagepub.co.uk.

SHOP
Abbey Home Farm's extensive onsite **Organic Farm Shop** is full of delicious food (much of which is grown just outside

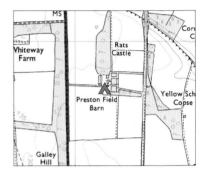

the door), as well as ethnicky clothes and even hand-made furniture – there's also a funky café in one corner; shop open Tue–Thur & Sat 9am–5pm, Fri 9am–6:30pm, Sun 11am–3pm (closed Mon); café open Tue–Thur 9am–4:30pm, Fri–Sat till 5pm, Sun 11am–4pm.

THERE AND AWAY
Train station: Kemble (7 miles) – London to Gloucester line. Bus no. 855 runs from the station to Cirencester, stopping at Stow Lodge, from where it's a 20-minute walk to the site.

OUT AND ABOUT
Corinium Museum, Cirencester (2¼ miles) – one of the nation's largest collections of Romano-British bits and bobs in what was the empire's second largest British town; adult £4.25, child (5–16) £2.25, family £11.50; open Mon–Sat 10am–5pm, Sun 2–5pm; 01285 655611; tinyurl.com/bb94d.
Cotswold Water Park (see Daneway Inn entry, p48)

open	Easter to Halloween
tiny campsites' rating	★★
friendliness	☺☺☺
cost	BP £££££, Couple £££££, Family £££££

GLOUCESTERSHIRE

One of the many joys of owning an immense organic farm is that you can put two campsites on it and neither of them need know of the other's existence. So it is at Abbey Home Farm, where the Chester-Masters' generous slice of Gloucestershire (a thumping two-and-a-half square miles' worth, to be precise) is home to woodland yurts, a 'normal' campsite and, a whole mile away, an amazing hideaway of a site.

The latter space consists of two small adjoining glades in the farm's Deer's Choice Wood, with space for about four medium-sized tents or two family-sized ones. Since the wood was only planted in 1991, the trees are still relatively small, giving campers the best of both worlds: sheltered seclusion and sunlight. To keep it secret and magical, the site has to be booked out in its entirety (£40 per night, minimum stay of two nights and a maximum number of eight people).

A tractor wheel serves as a brazier, and bags of coppiced ash firewood are available to buy at the farm shop, although you are encouraged to scavenge your own ('bring your own bow saw'). A discreet compost loo and a water tap complete the fixtures and fittings. From your base you are at liberty to roam the tracks and paths around the farm, taking in the nearby circle of standing stones (a modern creation, but none the poorer for it) or follow the signposted 30-minute farm walk. Just about the only thing you won't want to do, given that the farm shop and café can cater for your every need and then some, is leave.

15 Lyneham Lake

Churchill Heath
Kingham
Chipping Norton
Oxfordshire
OX7 6UJ

Mr and Mrs DJ Jakeman
01608 658491
Landranger: 163 (SP 269 224)

THE BASICS
Size: ¾ acre.
Pitches: 8 (0 hard standing).
Terrain: Flat.
Shelter: All round.
View: Down the lake.
Waterside: Yes.
Electric hook-ups: No.
Noise/Light/Olfactory pollution: No.

THE FACILITIES
Loos: 1M 1W. **Showers**: No.
Other facilities: No.
Stuff for children: No.
Recycling: No.

THE RULES
Dogs: On leads. **Fires**: No open fires; BBQs off grass. **Other**: No.

PUB LIFE
The Kingham Plough (free house; 1½ miles) – a posh pub/restaurant with tip-top locally sourced or foraged food (just don't call it nosh, scran or grub); open 12–'closing time' 7D; bar snacks (like Cotswold rarebit and sourdough soldiers, snails and mushrooms on toast) served 12–9:30pm 7D; restaurant open Mon–Sat 12–1:45pm & 7–8:45pm, Sun 12–2:30pm; 01608 658327; www.thekinghamplough.co.uk.
Or sample the **Chequers Inn** (free house), Churchill (1¾ miles) – another pub highly praised for its food (and posh too, though not quite as posh as the Plough) – booking strongly advised; open 12–midnight (coffee and tea served from 8am); food served Mon–Sat 12–2pm & 7–9:30pm, Sun 12–3pm & 7–9:30pm; 01608 659393.

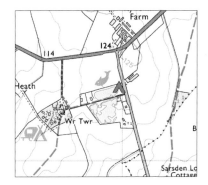

SHOP
Kingham PO (1½ miles) – sells 'almost everything'; open Mon–Fri 6:30am–7:30pm, Sat 7am–7pm, Sun (& BH) 8am–5pm; 01608 658235.

THERE AND AWAY
Train station: Kingham (1 mile) – London to Evesham line.

OUT AND ABOUT
Stow-on-the-Wold (6 miles) – often crammed to the gunwales with tourists, but catch it on a quiet day and you can appreciate why they flock to this attractive little Cotswolds town; www.visitcotswolds.co.uk.
Rollright Stones (8 miles) – a monarch and his court petrified by a witch (allegedly), the oldest stones having been put there by our Neolithic forebears some 5,000 years ago; adult £1, child 50p, U10 free; always open; 01608 642299; www.english-heritage.org.uk.

open	Easter to November
tiny campsites' rating	★ ★
friendliness	☺
cost	BP £, Couple £, Family £

What could be simpler? A lake, a few trees, some grass and a loo shed in the corner – all you have to do is supply the accommodation and a will to chill.

The only thing complicated about Lyneham Lake is finding it in the first place. Ordnance Survey maps conspire to confuse in this respect, since they continue to show caravan and tent symbols at a place that's just around the corner (and safely out of sight), which has been a cluster of holiday lodges for some time now. Put the postcode into your GPS and it too will have you heading for the lodges. To find the campsite without resorting to anguished gnashing of teeth, follow the main B4450 from Kingham towards Churchill, but turn off right, down Lyneham Road, and the entrance is on the right.

The area is a cyclist's paradise – there's nothing by way of steep hills, just plenty of quiet roads and oodles of small Cotswolds towns and villages desperate to be ridden to and pootled around in. A day's circular tour, for example, could take in Adlestrop (immortalised in a poem by Edward Thomas), Stow-on-the-Wold, Upper and Lower Slaughter, Fifield (a Domesday Book village) and Shipton-under-Wychwood for a pint at the Shaven Crown (www.theshavencrown.co.uk), a 700-year-old hostelry once used by the monks of Bruern Abbey as a hospice for the poor.

Back at the peaceful campsite, should your tummy fancy the look of any of the lake's fishy inhabitants, you can buy a day's fishing licence for £6 and try catching one or two for your supper.

Tadpole Bridge
Buckland Marsh
nr Faringdon
Oxfordshire
SN7 8RF

Environment Agency
Lock-keeper: Graham
01367 870218
www.visitthames.co.uk
Landranger: 164 (SP 322 001)

THE BASICS
Size: ⅓ acre.
Pitches: 5 (0 hard standing).
Terrain: Flat.
Shelter: Yes.
View: Across neighbouring fields.
Waterside: Yes, the Thames.
Electric hook-ups: No.
Noise/Light/Olfactory pollution: The muffled sloosh of water passing over the weir.

THE FACILITIES
Loos: 1U. **Showers**: No.
Other facilities: 2 picnic tables.
Stuff for children: No.
Recycling: No.

THE RULES
Dogs: Under control.
Fires: No open fires; BBQs off grass.
Other: Only walkers, cyclists and paddlers/rowers allowed (no cars).

PUB LIFE
The Trout Inn (free house), Tadpole Bridge (1 mile) – a pub that very much styles itself as a dining experience, hence award-winning and on the pricey side; open Mon–Sat 11:30am–3pm & 6–11pm, Sun 12–3:30pm & 6:30–10:30pm; food served 12–2pm & 7–9pm 7D; 01367 870382; www.trout-inn.co.uk. It also has a 20-pitch campsite should Rushey Lock be full.

SHOP
Scott's Budgens, Bampton (1½ miles by footpath) – a small supermarket; open Mon–Sat 8am–9pm, Sun 9am–9pm; 01993 850263.

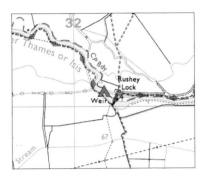

THERE AND AWAY
Train station: Oxford or Radley (both 15 miles) – Oxford is on many lines, while Radley lies between Oxford and Didcot Parkway. Stagecoach (www.stagecoachbus.com) runs buses from Oxford to Witney and Witney to Bampton.

OUT AND ABOUT
Kelmscott Manor, Kelmscott (9½ miles) – a listed Tudor farmhouse that was once home to William Morris of Arts and Crafts Movement fame; adult £8.50, child (8–16 years old) £4.25; open April to September Wed and 1st & 3rd Sat; 01367 252486; www.kelmscottmanor.org.uk.
Buscot Park, Faringdon (8¾ miles) – neoclassical house with some top-notch Pre-Raphaelite paintings; adult £7.50, child £3.75; open April to September Wed–Fri & some w/es 2–6pm; 01367 240786; NT site.
Thames Path (see Pinkhill Lock entry, p56, for details.)

open	April to October
tiny campsites' rating	★ ★
friendliness	☺☺
cost	BP ££, Couple ££, Family ££

Travel here on foot or bicycle from the nearest road and you are afforded the pleasure of a mile-long trip along a bank of the River Thames. Canoeists, kayakers and rowers have it even better, since they get to forge along the river itself, coming eye to eye with ducks, herons, geese and any other birdlife that happens to be swanning around.

Rushey Lock slumbers peacefully in its bucolic setting. There's a fine ivy-covered lock-keeper's house, a few small buildings housing whatever accoutrements are necessary for the execution of the lock-keeper's art, and the campsite – a small riverside field dotted with apple trees harbouring fruits of various crunchiness and flavour, and a loo in an unobtrusive building at the far end.

The distance from motorised road traffic lends the lock an atmosphere of unhurried tranquillity. Even the noise from the weir on the far side of the lock blends into a harmonious whole with the chirping of birds and whisper of leaves.

Footpaths extend not only along the river, but north towards the village of Bampton and south-east to Buckland, home of the extraordinary Palladian pile that is Buckland House (privately owned, but you get a cracking view of it from the road) and the 12th-century St Mary's Church, with its Crusader chest (a donation box for the Third Crusade).

Meanwhile, water-control buffs will note that Rushey sports a complete paddle and rymer weir, a system unchanged since its invention in the 13th century.

Eynsham
Witney
Oxfordshire
OX29 4JH

Environment Agency
Lock-keeper: Tim Brown
01865 881452
www.visitthames.co.uk
OS Landranger: 164 (SP 440 071)

THE BASICS
Size: ⅕ acre.
Pitches: 5 (0 hard standing).
Terrain: Flat.
Shelter: Under horse chestnut trees.
View: The river and a field beyond.
Waterside: Yes, the Thames.
Electric hook-ups: No.
Noise/Light/Olfactory pollution: The gushing of water through the weir.

THE FACILITIES
Loos: 1U. **Showers**: 1U (free).
Other facilities: No.
Stuff for children: No.
Recycling: No.

THE RULES
Dogs: On leads.
Fires: Open fires; BBQs off grass.
Other: The site is for walkers, cyclists and rowers/paddlers only. Campers must arrive during the lock-keeper's duty hours: April (9am–5pm), May (till 6:30pm), June to August (till 7pm), September (till 6pm).

PUB LIFE
The Talbot Inn (Arkell's), nr Eynsham (2 miles, mainly along Thames footpath) – recently renovated 18th-century pub with exposed beams, real ales and a sitting area outside overlooking a large stream (and, sadly, an oxygen works); open 7:30am–'very late' 7D; breakfast served 7:30–9am, lunch 12–2:30pm & dinner 6–9pm; 01865 881348; www.talbot-oxford.co.uk.

SHOP
Farmoor Stores (1 mile) – general store, bakery, newsagents and (in case you're

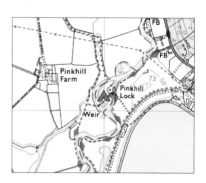

hankering after a bit of biltong) specialists in South African produce; Mon–Fri 7am–8pm, Sat 8am–5pm, Sun 9am–2pm; 01865 862656.

THERE AND AWAY
Train station: Oxford (4½ miles) – London to Birmingham line, among many others. Stagecoach (www.stagecoachbus.com) runs bus no. S1 from Oxford to Farmoor, stopping at Eynsham.

OUT AND ABOUT
Thames Path – just cross over the lock bridge to join the 184-mile trail stretching from source to sea; 01865 810224; www.nationaltrail.co.uk/Thamespath.
Farmoor Reservoir, just a field away, is the focus for a number of hides, a countryside walk and a wetland trail; 01865 863033.
Eynsham (pron. En-sham; 2 miles) is one of Britain's oldest settlements, having been around for at least 4,000 years, and home to nine pubs and a biennial open garden festival; www.eynsham.org.

open	April to September
tiny campsites' rating	★ ★ ★
friendliness	☺
cost	BP ££, Couple ££, Family ££

Time was when only wannabe musicians and artists lived on islands in the Thames. Nowadays, in contrast, the river's various isles, aits and eyots are colonised by a rather exclusive coterie who won't admit outsiders, no matter how bohemian their credentials. Happily, there is still a way to get your piece of fluvial island action, and for less than a tenner a night too. The island at Pinkhill Lock is just large enough to accommodate the lock-keeper's house and a small copse, one part of which, delineated by a couple of small signs with a simple tent on them, is the campsite.

Should you amble past the lock-keeper's abode, with its lovingly tended garden (one of the principal qualifications to be a lock-keeper is the possession of green fingers), and through a gap in the hedge, you'll find a new wooden shed inside which is a small bathroom containing a clean and modern shower and loo.

But that may be all the walking you'll get around to doing, for this is definitely a site for loafing around on. You can sit on the weir and become mesmerised by

the water falling headlong over it, keep watch for the pleasure boats and barges phutting up- and down-stream or merely marvel at the patterns the sun paints upon the surface of the river.

If you have a yen to be up and doing, there are several footpaths – including the Thames Path – leading off from the site, and a wildlife-rich wetland area right next door.

South-East England

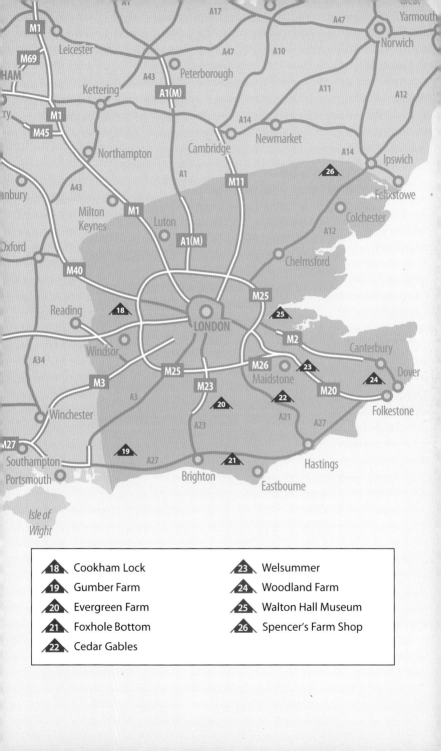

18	Cookham Lock	23	Welsummer
19	Gumber Farm	24	Woodland Farm
20	Evergreen Farm	25	Walton Hall Museum
21	Foxhole Bottom	26	Spencer's Farm Shop
22	Cedar Gables		

18 Cookham Lock

Odney Lane
Cookham
Maidenhead
Berkshire
SL6 9SR

Environment Agency
Lock-keeper: Adam Benge
☎ 01628 520752
🖥 www.visitthames.co.uk
OS Landranger: 175 (SU 905 855)

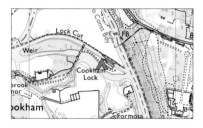

THE BASICS
Size: 2 x ¼ acre.
Pitches: Approx. 10 (0 hard standing).
Terrain: Flat.
Shelter: Some pitches.
View: Cliveden Cliffs.
Waterside: Yes, the Thames.
Electric hook-ups: No.
Noise/Light pollution: Occasional planes to/from Heathrow.

THE FACILITIES
Loos: 1U 1Disabled (radar key). **Showers**: 1 (£1 token from lock-keeper 'for 8 min.').
Other facilities: No.
Stuff for children: No.
Recycling: No.

THE RULES
Dogs: Yes, under control.
Fires: No open fires; BBQs off grass (brick pavers available).
Other: Camping only for those arriving by foot, bicycle or self-powered boat.

PUB LIFE
Bel and the Dragon (free house), Cookham (½ mile) – a cosy pub with a gastro menu; open Mon–Sat 11am–11pm, Sun till 10:30pm; food served Mon–Fri 12–2:30pm & 6–9:30pm; Sat 12–10pm; Sun till 8:30pm; 01628 521263; www.belandthedragon.co.uk.
Or for a pleasant 2-mile amble west along the Thames Path, there's the **Bounty** (free house) – a legendary maverick drinking hole not accessible by road; open 12–10:30pm(ish) 7D (October to Easter only open on w/es); food served 12–8pm 7D (when open); 01628 520056.

SHOP
Barnside Motors High Street, Cookham (¾ mile) – small news-tob-con; open Mon–Fri 8am–5:30pm; w/es till 3pm; 01628 525555.
Or **Country Store**, opposite Cookham station (2 miles) – mini supermarket; open Mon–Fri 6am–10pm, w/es 7am–9pm; 01628 522161.

THERE AND AWAY
Train station: Cookham (2 miles) – Marlow to Maidenhead line. The Arriva (www.arrivabus.co.uk) bus no. 37 runs from Cookham station to Cookham village.

OUT AND ABOUT
Stanley Spencer Gallery, Cookham (½ mile), showcase for the much loved local artist; adult £3, U16 free; open daily April to October 10:30am–5:30pm; November to March Thur–Sun 11am–4:30pm; 01628 471885; www.stanleyspencer.org.uk.
Cliveden, Taplow (3 miles) – once home to the 'fabulous Astors'; adult £9, child £4.50, family £20 (house and grounds); estate open daily March to October 11am–6pm; house open April to October Thur & Sun 3–5:30pm; 01628 605069; NT site.

open	April to end September
tiny campsites' rating	★ ★ ★
friendliness	☺ ☺ ☺
cost	BP ££, Couple ££, Family ££

Three cheers for whoever it was at the Environment Agency who thought it would be a good idea to use land at certain Thames locks for camping (see also Rushey Lock, p54, and Pinkhill Lock, p56). This site, at picturesque Cookham, is typical in its unfussy appearance and pleasingly unsophisticated facilities. There are two areas in which to pitch tents, a sheltered one near the lock-keeper's house, and a more scenic one on Sashes Island, wedged between the Thames and Hedsor Water. Birdlife abounds: visitors include kingfishers, red kites, parakeets, geese of all kinds and even the occasional hobby.

Toilets are in an eye-catching hexagonal wooden building, and there is a water tap at the back of the shower hut. An onsite refreshments kiosk also stocks bread, milk, tea and coffee (10am–5pm, every weekend from Easter to September – weather dependent – and daily during the school summer break).

To get to the lock, cross the bridge at the bottom of Odney Lane, take the

wide path to the weir and then follow the signs. It should be stressed that, as with all Thames lock sites, Cookham is not accessible by car. Furthermore, campers must arrive an hour before the weir gate is locked (April 5:30pm; May 6:30pm; June to August 7pm; September 6pm). There's a £10 deposit for the key.

Cookham village, though small, boasts one Chinese and three Indian restaurants, a smattering of pubs, and the unmissable Stanley Spencer Gallery (see opposite).

19 Gumber Farm

Estate Office
Slindon
West Sussex
BN18 0RG

National Trust
Keeper: Katie Archer
☎ 01243 814730
✉ katie.archer@nationaltrust.org.uk
🖥 tinyurl.com/mh5p9h
OS Landranger: 197 (SU 962 118)

THE BASICS
Size: ⅓ acre.
Pitches: Max. 35 people (0 hard standing).
Terrain: Pretty flat.
Shelter: From north.
View: Surrounding fields.
Waterside: No.
Electric hook-ups: No.
Noise/Light/Olfactory pollution: Dawn chorus: swallows, sparrows and wood pigeons in full voice.

THE FACILITIES
Loos: 4M 4W. **Showers**: 3M 3W (free).
Other facilities: Kitchen (inc. oven, kettle and washing-up area), drying room, horse paddock, bike shed.
Stuff for children: No.
Recycling: Everything.

THE RULES
Dogs: No.
Fires: Fire pit and BBQ available (charcoal £5/bag). **Other**: No vehicles on site; nearest parking 1½ miles.

PUB LIFE
The George (free house), Eartham (3 miles); open Mon–Fri 11am–11pm, w/es 12–11pm; food served Mon–Fri 12–2pm & 6:30–9pm, w/es 12–2:30pm & 6:30–9:30pm; 01243 814340; www.georgeinneartham.co.uk.

SHOP
Elm Tree Stores, Eastergate (4 miles) – a Tardis-like grocer's with more or less everything you might need, often at very reasonable prices; Mon–Sat 7:30am–7pm, Sun 8am–7pm; 01243 542117.

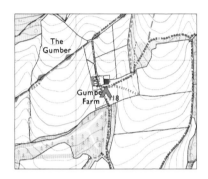

THERE AND AWAY
Train station: Amberley (5 miles) – London to Bognor Regis line. No onward bus route.

OUT AND ABOUT
Slindon village (1½ miles) – a fine example of what many Sussex villages would once have looked like, with some lovely flint and brick cottages; it also claims to be the birthplace of cricket and boasts (ahem) a famous autumn pumpkin display; www.slindon.com.
Arundel Castle (5 miles) – in a very pleasant hilltop location with 40 acres of grounds and gardens, Arundel hosts exquisite works of art, furniture, tapestries, china, sculpture, clocks and good old-fashioned suits of armour; adult £7–15, child £7, family £36–38; open April to October Tue–Sun (& BH & Mon in August) 10am–5pm; 01903 882173; www.arundelcastle.org.

open	April to October
tiny campsites' rating	★ ★ ★
friendliness	☺☺☺
cost	BP ££, Couple ££££, Family £££££

Run by the National Trust and situated on its 3,500-acre ewe-peppered Slindon Estate, Gumber Farm's campsite and bothy are an oasis of remoteness in the crowded south-east of England. The bothy (whose excellent facilities are available to campers) is a converted 19th-century flint barn in a large clearing within an enormous deer-filled wood. The small camping field is right outside it, as is the paddock, in which you may leave your mount should you have ridden in.

The irony is that a farm so lovely – it's surrounded by the sensuous curves of the South Downs and has been eulogised by none other than writer and historian Hilaire Belloc – is habitually used as just a brief stop-over by walkers and cyclists attempting either the South Downs Way or the Monarch's Way, both of which run close by. Were they to linger on the estate a little longer, they could visit Bronze Age burial mounds; a Neolithic flint knapping site; a section of the arrow-straight Stane Street (built by the Romans to link London and Chichester); and a Victorian folly. In World War II, a dummy airfield was laid out here (though only ever bombed once), and air raid shelters and other bits of fakery can still be seen today.

At night, the site becomes a star-gazer's paradise, with its huge sky untroubled by earthly lights. Come the morning and the same summer sky comes alive with swallows swooping around the plucky sparrows, who make their homes alongside them in the eaves of the bothy.

20 Evergreen Farm

West Hoathly Road
East Grinstead
West Sussex
RH19 4NE

Jane Warrener
01342 327720 & 07910993622
evergreenfarmcampsite@yahoo.co.u
Landranger: 187/198 (TQ 388 361)

THE BASICS
Size: ⅓ acre.
Pitches: 12 (0 hard standing).
Terrain: Mainly flat.
Shelter: Yes, all pitches are in woods.
View: Fields or East Grinstead, depending on pitch.
Waterside: No, but there is a nearby pond.
Electric hook-ups: No.
Noise/Light/Olfactory pollution: A solar-powered light by each pit.

THE FACILITIES
Compost Loos: 1U. **Showers**: No.
Other facilities: Free-range eggs for sale; maps of local walks can be borrowed.
Stuff for children: Many animals.
Recycling: Everything.

THE RULES
Dogs: At owners' discretion (max. 2 on site).
Fires: Open fires and BBQs in fire pit (£5 for 2 nights' worth of wood).
Other: No music (except acoustic instruments); visitors by arrangement.

PUB LIFE
The Old Mill (Whiting & Hammond), East Grinstead (¼ mile) – the old mill has, sadly, disappeared, but the stream's still there, as is a working replica of the water wheel; and you can take breakfast here in the summer too; open 10am–11pm ('and often later') 7D; food served Mon–Sat 12–9:30pm, Sun till 9pm; 01342 326341; www.theolddunningsmill.co.uk.

SHOP
Sunnyside PO, East Grinstead (¼ mile) – basics and, believe it or not, hand-made Peruvian necklaces; open Mon–Fri 6:15am–7pm, Sat 7:15am–7pm, Sun till noon; 01342 323319.

THERE AND AWAY
Train station: East Grinstead (2¾ miles) – London to East Grinstead line. The Metrobus (www.metrobus.co.uk) no. 84 runs from East Grinstead to Saint Hill, very close to the site.

OUT AND ABOUT
Weir Wood Reservoir (1 mile) – the Sussex Border Path (www.sussexborderpath.co.uk) runs alongside this 280-acre lake, which fair teems with birdlife; www.weirwood.me.uk.
Standen (¼ mile) – a gorgeous Victorian house and showcase for the Arts and Crafts Movement; adult £7.38, child £3.68, family £18.42 (the National Trust calculates entrance fees by throwing a lot of numbers up in the air and seeing how they fall); open mid March to October Wed–Sun 11am–4:30pm (Wed–Mon in August); 01342 323029; NT site.

open	All year (weather dependent)
tiny campsites' rating	★ ★ ★
friendliness	☺ ☺ ☺
cost	BP £££, Couple £££££, Family £££££

Who would have thought that it was possible to sample the delights of wild camping so close to London? All right, admittedly this is wild camping on private grounds, but it's still not bad for a site slap-bang in the middle of commuterland. Right next to the town immortalised in Alan Ayckbourn's *The Norman Conquests*, the woods at Evergreen seem so far removed from the hurly-burly of the capital that one could almost imagine that it no longer exists.

Excitingly, visitors are whisked off into the 10-acre wood on a trailer towed by a quad bike, to take their pick from pitches that range from the ultra-secluded to the moderately sociable. There are no standpipes but a large canister of drinking water is supplied, while the loo is a short walk away. Open fires are de rigueur; come in October and you can gather chestnuts and roast them. There's also a discount for anyone arriving by public transport or under their own steam.

The sheep, pigs, goats, chickens, ducks, horses and ponies on Evergreen Farm (which is no longer actually a farm) are pets (yep, even the pigs) and accompanied children can meet up with them for some fussing/petting interaction on request.

Close by there's Deers Leap Park, 240 acres devoted to mountain biking (¼ mile; www.deersleapbikes.co.uk), the Bluebell Railway (Kingscote station; 1¾ miles; www.bluebell-railway.co.uk); and Ashdown Forest (6 miles; www.ashdownforest.org) where Winnie the Pooh once hunted heffalumps.

Foxhole Bottom Campsite
Seven Sisters Country Park
Exceat
Seaford
East Sussex
BN25 4AD

Seven Sisters Visitor Services Team

01323 870280

sevensisters@southdowns-aonb.gov.uk

www.sevensisters.org.uk

Landranger: 199 (TV 523 982)

THE BASICS
Size: ⁴/₅ acre.
Pitches: 20 (0 hard standing).
Terrain: Very gently sloping.
Shelter: Yes.
View: Surrounding fields.
Waterside: No.
Electric hook-ups: No.
Noise/Light/Olfactory pollution: No.

THE FACILITIES
Loos: 4U 1Disabled (radar key). **Showers** (solar): 1U (free).
Other facilities: Washing-up area, picnic tables, cooking area, bike shed.
Stuff for children: No.
Recycling: Cans, bottles.

THE RULES
Dogs: If well behaved.
Fires: No fires or BBQs.
Other: Campers must be 21 or over or, if in a group, have at least one person over the age of 21 staying with them; groups of 4 or more must book in advance; no alcohol.

PUB LIFE
The Golden Galleon (free house), Exceat Bridge (¾ mile); a busy pub with a large beer garden; open Mon–Sat 12–11pm, Sun 12–10:30pm; food served Mon–Sat 12–10pm, Sun till 9:30pm; 01323 892247. Slightly further afield, but well worth the effort to get to (you can walk on footpaths most of the way) is the ancient low-beamed **Tiger Inn** (Beachy Head Brewery), East Dean (3 miles); open 11am–11pm 7D; food served 12–3pm & 6–9pm 7D; 01323 423209.

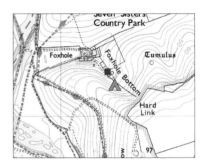

SHOP
Nearby Seaford town has a wide range of shops including a **Co-op** (2¼ miles) – small supermarket; open Mon–Sat 7am–10pm, Sun 8am–10pm; 01323 892482.

THERE AND AWAY
Train station: Seaford (2½ miles) – Seaford to Lewes line. The frequent bus nos.12 and 12A, run by Brighton and Hove (www.buses.co.uk), go from Seaford to Seven Sisters Country Park.

OUT AND ABOUT
The South Downs Way passes the campsite's front door on its way to Beachy Head and Eastbourne; free; always open; www.nationaltrail.co.uk/Southdowns.
Alfriston (4 miles) – a beautiful, ancient village containing St Andrew's Church, 'the Cathedral of the South Downs', and the Clergy House, the National Trust's first ever property; adult £3.90, child £1.95, family £9.75; open daily (except Tue & Fri) in summer, 10:30am–5pm; 01323 870001; NT site.

open	April to October
tiny campsites' rating	★ ★ ★
friendliness	☺☺
cost	BP £, Couple ££, Family £££

Hidden away in a cleft between the hills, Foxhole Bottom (no sniggering at the back) offers a rare opportunity to camp inside a country park. Not just any old country park, either: Seven Sisters is where you'll find some fantastically bumpy South Downs; a snaking river sliding off into the sea; a shingle beach; a wetland reserve for birds; and those national treasures, the Seven Sisters cliffs.

The campsite consists of a simple oblong field in front of a cavernous Sussex barn that serves as a camping barn. The modern facilities – including a covered kitchen area in which to set up one's stove – form an attractive grassy courtyard at the back of the building.

Foxhole Bottom is aimed at backpackers and cyclists (there's £1 off if you arrive under your own steam), so it's a small-tents-only site. Thus, there's a marked absence of those vast pavilions that blot out the sun and which, one suspects, not only have four bedrooms and a loft extension but a wine cellar too.

No vehicles are allowed in the country park, keeping it blissfully free of traffic and its accompanying noise. It's a level mile-long walk into the site from the car park (£5 overnight charge) or the bus stop, which adds to the sense that here you are in a world of your own. Indeed, there's so much natural beauty to enjoy in the park that it's quite possible to spend a weekend here without ever feeling the need to leave it.

Hastings Road
Flimwell
Wadhurst
Kent
TN5 7QA

Mrs Morgan
01892 890566 & 07703 024579
jo@cedargables.wanadoo.co.uk
www.caravanandcampingsites.co.uk
Landranger: 188 (TQ 695 335)

THE BASICS
Size: ¾ acre.
Pitches: 30 (0 hard standing).
Terrain: Gently sloping.
Shelter: Trees all round.
View: No.
Waterside: No.
Electric hook-ups: 11.
Noise/Light/Olfactory pollution: Close
to busy A-road.

THE FACILITIES
Loos: 2M 2W. **Showers**: 2M 2W (50p token
for 'about 5 min.').
Other facilities: Info shed with settee,
books, mobile charger, 2 washing-up sinks,
kettle, fridge/freezer, hairdryer.
Stuff for children: Mini adventure
playground.
Recycling: Glass, paper.

THE RULES
Dogs: On leads. **Fires**: Use site's own BBQ
(£5 bags of charcoal available). **Other**: No.

PUB LIFE
Globe and Rainbow (free house),
Kilndown (1¼ miles) – smart pub/
restaurant serving locally sourced food,
with occasional live music; films shown
on alternate Wed from September to May;
open Sun–Mon 12–8pm, Tue–Sat till 11pm;
lunch served Mon–Sat 12–2:30pm, Sun
12:30–3:30pm, dinner served Tue–Thur
7–9pm, Fri–Sat till 9:30pm; 01892 890803.

SHOP
Victoria House PO, Lamberhurst
(2¼ miles) – small grocer's and off licence,
basic fruit & veg, newspapers; open

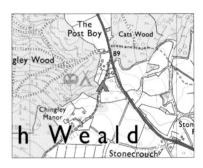

Mon–Thur 6am–7pm, Fri–Sat till 8pm,
Sun 7am–4pm; 01892 890278.

THERE AND AWAY
Train station: Wadhurst or Frant (both
6 miles) – London to Hastings line. No
onward bus service to the site.

OUT AND ABOUT
Bewl Water (¾ mile) – walkers, mountain
bikers and horse-riders can all tackle the
13-mile track around the reservoir; free;
always open; www.bewlwater.org.
Scotney Castle (1¾ miles) – Victorian
country house, gardens and 14th-century
ruined castle; adult £8.50, child £4.25,
family £21.50; open March to October
Wed–Sun 11am–4pm (for winter opening
times see website); 01892 893820; NT site.
Bedgebury Forest (2 miles) – cycle trails,
mountain biking, walking, the National
Pinetum and Go Ape (0845 6439215;
www.goape.co.uk) hire-wire adventure;
free entry to forest (car park charge);
open daily 8am–7pm; 01580 879820;
www.forestry.gov.uk/bedgebury.

open	All year
tiny campsites' rating	★ ★
friendliness	☺☺
cost	BP ££, Couple £££, Family £££

If you have a penchant for travelling with the work of an earlier generation of cartographers, you won't find Bewl Water on your map because the picturesque reservoir only came into being in 1975 (when the River Bewl was stopped up). You will have a great time reaching it from Cedar Gables, however; an ancient sunken track spears its way down there, passing fields of wheat and bushes laden with blackcurrants. A left turn at the shore will take you to a bench boasting a view right down the length of the reservoir which, on Wednesday evenings and weekends, is dotted with tiny sail boats, and echoes to the heavy metronomic thud of four-man sculls.

Back at the extremely well-maintained campsite, a gently sloping field sliced in two by a fence provides space for campers on one side and games on the other. Picnic tables grace the well-mown lawn where, at the top end, sweet chestnut trees provide shade from the sun on hot days. It's a shame that the birdsong and the soughing of the breeze in the branches has to compete with the swish of traffic from the A21, but at least the road is hidden from view.

All the loos and showers have been completely revamped, while a small shed houses innumerable leaflets plugging local attractions, a fridge/ freezer for campers' use and a few shelves of airport novels to read (or exchange for any airport novels you may have accidentally brought along yourself). There's also a three-piece suite on which to cosy up and devour them.

23 Welsummer

Welsummer Camping
Chalk House
Lenham Road
Kent
ME17 1NQ

Med and Laura Benagounne
01622 844048
bakehousemail@yahoo.co.uk
www.welsummer.moonfruit.co.uk
OS Landranger: 189 (TQ 866 505)

THE BASICS
Size: ³/₅ acre and 6 tiny pitches in wood.
Pitches: 20 (0 hard standing).
Terrain: Flat.
Shelter: Trees on 2 sides.
View: No.
Waterside: No.
Electric hook-ups: No.
Noise/Light/Olfactory pollution: Distant rumble of M20 traffic.

THE FACILITIES
Loos: 2U. **Showers**: 2U (free).
Other facilities: Shop selling basic foodstuffs, camping supplies, the smallholding's own free-range eggs and organically grown veg; hot drinks and hot snacks served all day.
Stuff for children: Trees to climb, 'places to hide'.
Recycling: Everything.

THE RULES
Dogs: Max. 3 on site at any one time.
Fires: Most pitches have a fire pit (firewood £3).
Other: Acoustic instruments and fireside singing positively encouraged, but radios and other electronica frowned upon; no looting the woods for firewood.

PUB LIFE
The Pepperbox Inn (Shepherd Neame), Windmill Hill, nr Ulcombe (¾ mile) – food comes highly recommended (no U14s allowed inside, but there is a beer garden); open Mon–Fri 11am–3pm & 6–11pm, Sat 12–11pm, Sun till 4pm; food served Mon–Sat 12–2pm & 7–9:30pm, Sun 12–3pm; 01622 842558; www.thepepperboxinn.co.uk.

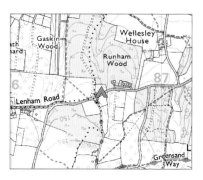

SHOP
Lenham Village Store (2¼ miles) – small grocer's and off licence; open Mon–Thur 8am–8pm, Fri–Sat till 9pm, Sun 10am–6pm; 01622 858255. Lenham is an attractive little market town whose shops include a deli and a chemist.

THERE AND AWAY
Train station: Lenham or Harrietsham (both 2 miles) – Maidstone to Ashford line. No onward bus service to the site.

OUT AND ABOUT
Leeds Castle (3¾ miles) – sheer stone-fortress perfection; adult £16.50, child £9.50; open daily April to September 10:30am–5:30pm, October to March till 4pm; 01622 765400; www.leeds-castle.com.
Biddenden Vineyards (11 miles) – wine tasting and 22 acres of vines to admire; free; open Mon–Sat 10am–5pm, Sun & BH 11am–5pm; 01580 291726; www.biddendenvineyards.com.

open	April to October
tiny campsites' rating	★★★
friendliness	☺☺☺
cost	BP £££, Couple ££££, Family £££££

If you're one of those people who lie awake at night fretting over whether you prefer camping in a field or in a wood – there's no shame in it, there are millions of us out there – you'll be relieved to learn that there is a select posse of sites that offers both, one of which is Welsummer.

On arrival, the site appears quite conventional: a short track off a minor road leads up to two small, flat camping fields. However, go through an unobtrusive gate underneath a

beech tree and you enter a dense dark wood harbouring half-a-dozen pitches, which can only be described as naturalistic – the owners, Laura and Med, may have to point them out to you before you realise where they are. This is quite deliberate as Laura used to camp in these woods as a child and her aim is to offer others a taste of the joys she experienced back then.

Situated on a smallholding with chickens roaming around a copse, bees zipping in and out of hives, and a miniature orchard containing native English apples, Welsummer is a laidback campsite that wears its quirky touches lightly (rainbow-coloured windsock, anyone?). Prepare to make friends here, too. This is the sort of place where meals are shared with strangers, especially with those who make the schoolboy error of not lighting their fire early enough in the evening to cook their jacket potatoes by a reasonable hour, so end up stuffing themselves with that haute cuisine of al fresco cooking: the half-incinerated marshmallow.

Walderchain
Barham
Kent
CT4 6NS

📧 Mrs Bennett
📞 01227 831892
✉ denise.longhurst@hotmail.com
🗺 Landranger: 189 (TR 207 484)

THE BASICS
Size: ¼ acre & pitches in a wood.
Pitches: 5 in field, 7 in wood (0 hard standing).
Terrain: Flat.
Shelter: Yes.
View: No.
Waterside: No.
Electric hook-ups: No.
Noise/Light/Olfactory pollution: No.

THE FACILITIES
Loos: 2U. **Showers**: 1 (free).
Other facilities: No.
Stuff for children: A tree swing, the woods.
Recycling: Paper, glass, cans.

THE RULES
Dogs: If well behaved.
Fires: Yes, in braziers. **Other**: No.

PUB LIFE
The Duke of Cumberland (Punch Taverns), Barham (1 mile) – a lovely old pub with a reputation for food and a beer festival on the first w/e of July; open Mon–Fri 12–3pm & 5:30–11pm (Fri till midnight), w/es 12–midnight; food served 12–2:30pm & 6–8:30pm 7D; 01227 831396; www.dukeofcumberland.co.uk.

SHOP
Barham PO (1 mile); it's a Portakabin, so just the basics and newspapers; Mon–Tue, Thur–Fri 8am–1pm & 2–5:30pm, Wed & w/e mornings only.

THERE AND AWAY
Train station: Snowdown (3½ miles) – Canterbury to Dover line. The Stagecoach

(www.stagecoachbus.com) bus no. 89 runs from Snowdown station to Barham.

OUT AND ABOUT
Howletts Wild Animal Park, Bekesbourne, nr Canterbury (8 miles) – set up by the late John Aspinall to protect endangered species and return them to their native environment; adult £16.95, U17 £12.95, U3 free; open summer 10am–6pm (last admission 4:30pm), winter till 5pm (last admission 3:30pm); 01227 721286; www.totallywild.net/howletts.
Canterbury Cathedral (10 miles) – the mothership of the Anglican Church and a glorious building to boot; adult £7.50, child £6.50 (or attend a service for free); open summer 9am–5pm, winter till 4:30pm; 01227 762862; www.canterbury-cathedral.org.

open	March to September
tiny campsites' rating	★ ★
friendliness	☺☺
cost	BP £, Couple ££, Family £££

There are some campsites that somehow capture the very essence of camping. The site at Woodland Farm is a simple, sunny, semi-circular clearing in a wood. A dainty apple tree stands in the middle, while a faded green clapperboard hut, containing two super-clean loos and one shower, tucks itself into the trees at one side. With thick woodland all around, the site forms its own little universe.

A dark track leading into the woods promises even greater seclusion. Rough and ready pitches can be found wherever the trees thin sufficiently enough to put a tent up. There's a refreshingly relaxed attitude to the location of pitches too, so you can go anywhere you can find space.

The regulars here often turn the clearing into a venue for all manner of ad hoc games you won't find represented in the Olympics, including a sort of raquetless tennis played with a football and two deckchairs. Should the weather become too hot or wet there are some chairs, tables and a bench in a shelter, the architecture of which does its best to defy description: imagine an over-sized Anderson shelter done in the style of a tropical beach hut. But perhaps the greatest innovation on the site is its braziers. The large metal cylinders once served as washing machine tumblers. The owner's son-in-law mends washing machines, and when they can't be mended, they turn up here.

In the evening, a stroll through the wood and across an adjoining field brings you to Barham, over the far side of which is its greatest treasure, the Duke of Cumberland pub.

Walton Hall Road
Linford
Stanford-le-Hope
Essex
SS17 0RH

Mr Frank Wood
01375 671874
info@waltonhall.com
www.waltonhallmuseum.com
Landranger: 177 (TQ 676 801)

THE BASICS
Size: 1 acre.
Pitches: 25 (25 hard standing).
Terrain: Mostly flat.
Shelter: A few pitches.
View: No.
Waterside: No.
Electric hook-ups: 20.
Noise/Light pollution: Some noise from road; light on outside loo.

THE FACILITIES
Loos: 2M 2W. **Showers**: 1U (50p for 'plenty of time').
Other facilities: None.
Stuff for children: A large adventure playground area, an art room.
Recycling: Everything.

THE RULES
Dogs: No. **Fires**: 2 dedicated sites for BBQs, otherwise no. **Other**: No.

PUB LIFE
The Ship (free house), East Tilbury (2½ miles) – with a separate restaurant that is very popular at w/es, so be sure to book; open 12–11pm 7D; food served 12–2:30pm & 6–9pm 7D; 01375 843041.

SHOP
Lloyds Linford Stores (1 mile) – groceries, newspapers and a small deli counter; open Mon–Sat 5:30am–8pm, Sun 6:30am–7:30pm; 01375 675606. The small town of Stanford-le-Hope (2 miles) has a smattering of shops.

THERE AND AWAY
Train station: East Tilbury (2 miles) –

London to Southend line. The Clintona Minicoaches bus no. 374 runs from East Tilbury to Linford.

OUT AND ABOUT
Walton Hall Museum (right next door) adult £4, child £2; open April to October Thur–Sun (and most days in school holidays) 10am–5pm.
Coalhouse Fort (2¾ miles) – entrance at the bottom of Margaret Road, East Tilbury; free; open all the time; 01375 844203; www.coalhousefort.co.uk.
Stanford Marshes (2 miles) – nature reserve boasting a wide variety of plants, animals and birdlife in a setting of reed beds, salt marsh and mudflats. Also a rare piece of Thames riverside open to the public. Entrance on Wharf Road, Stanford-le-Hope; free; open all the time.

open	All year
tiny campsites' rating	★ ★
friendliness	☺
cost	BP ££, Couple ££, Family £££

A rare treat of a campsite with a winning combination of entertainment and education: the Walton Hall Museum boasts its own motor roller collection; a 17th-century barn full of old domestic and farmyard utensils; a café serving drinks and sandwiches; a bakery (bake your own bread in a 100-year-old oven); a printers' workshop; a gift shop; some rabbits, hamsters and guinea pigs; a metal-detector shop (no campsite should be without one) and even its own ghost (and ghost hunting events). And if this isn't enough, entry is free to those booking a stay of over two nights.

It's a pity the camping ground itself isn't a little more aesthetically pleasing (though motorhomers will no doubt look fondly on all the hard standing should it rain), but if a bit of Essex shtick is your thing, you'll be in seventh heaven. An inner enclosure (five pitches) leads to an outer field beyond, which is more exposed, but blessed with views of a farm that appears to specialise in growing pylons. However, things do take a considerable turn for the better at the picnic lawn, a lovely sheltered area guarded by a carved wooden Green Man, while the adventure playground has the handsome black barn as a backdrop.

Nearby Coalhouse Fort is an impressive stronghold completed in 1874 by Victorians living in mortal fear of French ironclad ships. You can wander around the grounds at any time, while on open and special event days there are guided tours that include the military and aviation museums. There's also a tea room and shop.

Wickham Fruit Farm
Wickham St Paul
Halstead
Essex
CO9 2PX

Paul and Liz Spencer
01787 269476
info@spencersfarmshop.co.uk
www.spencersfarmshop.co.uk
Landranger: 155 (TL 833 360)

THE BASICS
Size: ⅓ acre.
Pitches: Variable, but a max. of 5 caravans (1 hard standing).
Terrain: Flat.
Shelter: Yes.
View: No.
Waterside: No.
Electric hook-ups: 8.
Noise/Light/Olfactory pollution: No.

THE FACILITIES
Loos: 1U. **Showers**: 1U (£2 per night).
Other facilities: CDP.
Stuff for children: PYO fruit, an old farm tractor to sit on.
Recycling: Bottles, tins, plastic.

THE RULES
Dogs: If well behaved.
Fires: BBQs allowed off grass; go beyond into paddock for open fires.
Other: No.

PUB LIFE
The Victory Inn (independent), Wickham St Paul (¼ mile) – extremely popular due to its highly rated food, so do book; open Mon–Thur 11am–11pm, Fri–Sat 11–1am, Sun 12–11pm; lunch served Mon–Sat 12–2:30pm, Sun till 4pm; dinner Mon–Thur 6–9:30pm, Fri–Sat till 10pm; 01787 269364; www.thevictoryinn.com.

SHOP
Spencer's Farm Shop (on site) – full of really tasty goodies, local wines and organic beers, as well as milk and bread; Mon–Sat 9am–5:30pm, Sun 10am–4pm (café 10am–4pm 7D).

THERE AND AWAY
Train station: Sudbury (4 miles) – Sudbury to Marks Tey line. One bus an hour (no. 11, 12 & 13) runs from Sudbury to the farm.

OUT AND ABOUT
Hedingham Castle, Castle Hedingham (4¼ miles) – a quite astonishing Norman keep with a tremendous banqueting hall, exquisite grounds and frequent special events such as jousting tournaments; adult £5, child £3.50, U5 free, family £17 (try not to swoon at the massive discount); open mid April to October Mon–Thur 11am–4pm, Sun 10am–5pm, (some selected dates have restricted opening: see website); 01787 460261; www.hedinghamcastle.co.uk.
Dedham (16 miles) – a village on the River Stour at the epicentre of Constable country. Georgian houses and craggy inns abound, while the 15th-century church and the highly paintable water meadows on the edge of the village are also worth a gander.

open	All year (weather dependent)
tiny campsites' rating	✶✶
friendliness	☺☺☺
cost	BP ££, Couple ££, Family ££

ESSEX

Poor old Essex: forever enshrined in the nation's consciousness as a county of furry dice, Chingford WAGs and Wayne and Waynettas in matching shellsuits. In reality a great deal of the county, particularly as it ambles across gently undulating fields towards the Suffolk border, is chock full of rustic villages whose taste no one in their right mind would question.

Such is the case of Wickham St Paul, on the outskirts of which you'll find Spencer's Farm Shop, a pick-your-own establishment with a café and, as the name imparts, a farm shop. The small campsite they run is very much part of the farm: polytunnels harbouring thousands of luscious strawberries run the length of one side, and it's a very strong-willed camper indeed who can spend a day here without succumbing to the temptation of grabbing a punnet in the shop and picking-their-own.

The loo/shower is attached to the shop (though with 24-hour access for campers), and is a 200-metre stroll from the campsite, passing all manner of crops awaiting amateur harvest, including rhubarb, plums, apples, blackcurrants, boysenberries, tummelberries, Buckingham tayberries and humble blackberries (though these also grow wild in the hedge and are free). Handily, there are some picnic tables outside the café where you can feast on the banquet of fruit you have picked (though do pay for it first).

It's a shame about the electricity pylons that march through the farm (is there any other by-product of modern life that has disfigured the countryside more?) but, thankfully, they're barely noticeable from the campsite itself.

East Anglia

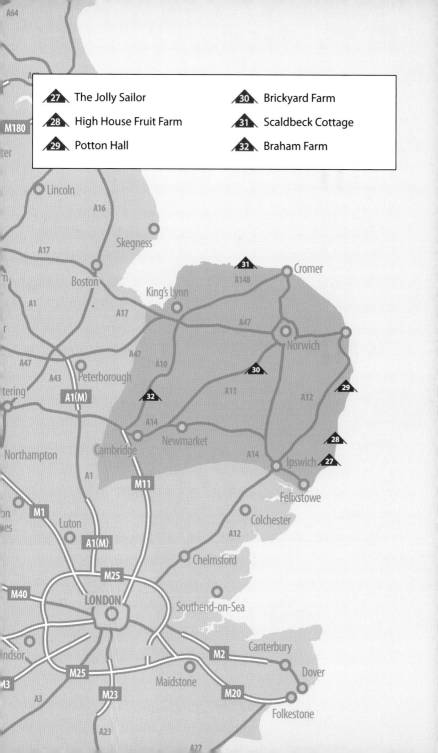

Quay Street
Orford
Woodbridge
Suffolk
IP12 2NU

Gordon Williams
01394 450243
hello@thejollysailor.net
www.thejollysailor.net
Landranger: 156/169 (TM 423 496)

THE BASICS

Size: ¹/₁₀ acre.
Pitches: 6 (0 hard standing).
Terrain: Slightly sloping.
Shelter: All round.
View: The sea wall and Havergate Island from the beer garden.
Waterside: No, but the River Ore is only 50 metres away.
Electric hook-ups: No.
Noise/Light/Olfactory pollution: Beer garden next door.

THE FACILITIES

Loos: A wet room with shower & toilet (open 24 hours) & 1M 2W in pub.
Other facilities: Brand new kitchenette including a fridge, washing-up area, 2 electric rings, kettle, microwave and breakfast bar.
Stuff for children: Swings, trampoline, crabbing nets, Wendy house, Shrimp the cat.
Recycling: Everything, including food waste.

THE RULES

Dogs: If well behaved. **Fires**: No open fires; braziers supplied for BBQs. **Other**: No.

PUB LIFE

The Jolly Sailor (Adnams; 10 metres) – mentioned in just about every good food/drink guide on the planet; open Mon–Fri 11am–3pm & 6–11:30pm, w/es 12–midnight; food served 12–3pm & 6–9pm 7D.

SHOP

Orford Supply Stores (¼ mile) – a grocer's, deli and café all rolled into one; open

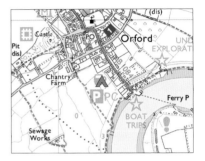

Mon–Sat 8:30am–5:30pm (closes 1pm on Wed), Sun 10am–1pm; 01394 450219.

THERE AND AWAY

Train station: Wickham Market and Melton (both around 9 miles) – London to Lowestoft line. Bus no. 71, run by Far East Travel, goes from Melton to Orford.

OUT AND ABOUT

Orford Castle (½ mile) – impressive 12th-century 18-sided keep built by Henry II; adult £5, child £2.50, family £12.50; open daily April to June & September 10am–5pm, July & August till 6pm, October to March Thur–Mon 10am–4pm; 01394 450472; www.english-heritage.org.uk.
Orford Ness – the experimental weapons facility turned nature reserve; access by ferry only (10am–5pm) from Orford Quay (100 metres); adult entry & ferry return £6.90, child £3.45, U3 free; 01728 648024; NT site. Other river trips available on Regardless (07900 230579; www. orfordrivertrips.co.uk) and Lady Florence (07831 698298; www.lady-florence.co.uk).

open	All year
tiny campsites' rating	★ ★
friendliness	☺ ☺
cost	BP £££, Couple £££, Family ££££

If the Jolly Sailor were the setting for a novel, critics would pounce on it as being too clichéd for words. 'A 16th-century smugglers' inn with exposed beams taken from wrecked shipping, and inhabited by a ghost?' they would splutter. 'The place where an escaped lady horse-thief is dramatically re-arrested?' they would thunder, before shuffling off to mutter at something else.

Except, of course, it's all true: smugglers abounded, the horse thief was a certain 18-year-old Margaret Catchpole who was subsequently packed off to Australia (her 'wanted' poster is in the snug bar) and the ghost made its most recent appearance five years ago (though there are regular ghost hunting nights held at the pub to check if it's still around). What's more, a sea shanty band plays once a month on a Saturday night. If you want to be transported to a time when they did things very differently indeed, the Jolly Sailor is the place to come.

The campsite is a long thin apple orchard surrounded by a high hedge. Not only is this a very private and sheltered area, but the trees are so close that, aside from in a mini-glade at the far end, there's no room for cathedral-sized tents. However, since there are only six pitches in the orchard, there's loads of space in which to stretch out horizontally.

Orford itself was once a prominent port, but now seems content to see out its days as a graceful fishing village.

Sudbourne
Woodbridge
Suffolk
IP12 2BL

Piers and Suvi Pool
01394 450263
campsite@high-house.co.uk
www.high-house.co.uk
OS Landranger: 156 (TM 431 527)

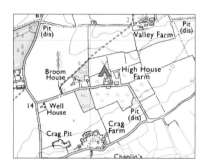

THE BASICS
Size: ½ acre.
Pitches: Max. 15 people (0 hard standing).
Terrain: Flat.
Shelter: Yes.
View: No.
Waterside: No.
Electric hook-ups: No.
Noise/Light/Olfactory pollution: During the day there's the merry toing and froing of farm vehicles.

THE FACILITIES
Loos: 1M 1W. **Showers**: No.
Other facilities: Washing-up area, kettle.
Stuff for children: No. **Recycling**: No.

THE RULES
Dogs: No. **Fires**: No open fires; self-contained BBQs only. **Other**: All stays must be booked in advance.

PUB LIFE
In Orford (2 miles) there are several cracking options including the **King's Head** (Adnams) – a 13th-century pub serving real ales and food made with locally sourced ingredients; open Mon–Fri 11:30am–3:30pm & 6–11pm, Sat 11:30am–1130pm, Sun 12–10:30pm; lunch served 12–2:30pm 7D, dinner Mon–Sat 6:30–9pm; 01394 450271; www.thekingsheadorford.co.uk. There's also the **Jolly Sailor** (see p80) – the new boy on the block (it's only been there since the 16th century).

SHOP
Orford Supply Stores (2 miles; see the Jolly Sailor entry, p80)

THERE AND AWAY
Train station: Wickham Market (8 miles) – London to Lowestoft line. From there, take the train to Woodbridge to catch Far East Travel's bus no. 71 to Sudbourne.

OUT AND ABOUT
Orford Castle (2 miles) – (see the Jolly Sailor entry, p80).
Snape Maltings, nr Aldeburgh (4¾ miles) – former barley-malting works that now offers a high-class programme of concert hall events (particularly during the Aldeburgh Festival); boat trips and walks along the River Alde; delectable eateries and a slew of fancy shops; 01728 688303; www.snapemaltings.co.uk.

open	End March to end October
tiny campsites' rating	✷ ✷
friendliness	☺☺
cost	BP ££, Couple ££, Family ££££

Too often campsites on farms give the impression of having been not just an afterthought but a thought that has occurred long after the afterthought. If you could hear the farmers' thoughts, they would be thinking, 'Any scrap of land will do, no matter how unsuitable it may be for camping'.

The obverse appears to have taken place at High House Fruit Farm, where the very best spot for camping has been selected: a flat field protected from the channel winds by attractive trees all round, and yet open to the sun. It's also just a hop and a step from the facilities, housed in a farm building. The trees are, in turn, surrounded by apple orchards, which somehow give the place a summery feel whatever the weather.

The 110-acre farm is primarily one on which cattle graze, but there's still plenty of room for the apple trees as well as for the rhubarb, gooseberries, currants, loganberries, blackberries, cherries and plums, many of which you can harvest yourself (it's a pick-your-own farm too: punnets and measuring scales available in the farm's tiny shop, where you'll also find bottles of home-made apple juice, preserves and a small selection of veg).

Peace and tranquillity are the order of the day. The farm itself is far from anywhere in particular, and the maximum number of people allowed on the site is a mere 15, so there's always plenty of room to spread out. Please do note, however, that advance booking is mandatory, so don't just rock up here, empty punnet in hand and hope.

Blythburgh Road
Westleton
Suffolk
IP17 3EF

Jeremy and Helen Hayes
01728 648265
OS Landranger: 156 (TM 453 710)

THE BASICS
Size: ⁶/₇ acre.
Pitches: 10 (0 hard standing).
Terrain: Flat.
Shelter: On 3 sides.
View: On to the next field with woods beyond.
Waterside: River Dunwich (but you'll have to look for it).
Electric hook-ups: No.
Noise/Light/Olfactory pollution: No.

THE FACILITIES
Loos: No. **Showers**: No.
Other facilities: CDP.
Stuff for children: No. **Recycling**: No.

THE RULES
Dogs: If well behaved.
Fires: No open fires; BBQs off grass.
Other: No children.

PUB LIFE
The Ship at Dunwich (2¼ miles) – a pub with a reputation for good food, so it's a good idea to book; open Mon–Sat 11am–11pm, Sun 12–10:30pm; food served 12–3pm & 6–9pm 7D; 01728 648219; www.shipatdunwich.co.uk.

SHOP
Lincoln's Village PO, Westleton (1½ miles) – grocer's, fruit & veg and off licence; open Mon–Sat 8:30am–1pm & 2–5:30pm (Wed mornings only), Sun 9am–noon; 01728 648216.

THERE AND AWAY
Train station: Darsham (3¾ miles) – Ipswich to Lowestoft line. Wayland's

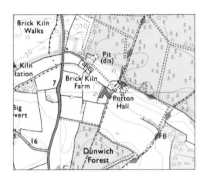

Minibuses' (www.waylandminibusservices.co.uk) no. 196 runs occasionally from Darsham to Westleton.

OUT AND ABOUT
Dunwich Museum (2¼ miles) – witness the curious case of the proud city that the sea turned into a small village (with a heath teeming in wildlife); entry by donation; see website for varying opening times; 01728 648796; www.dunwichmuseum.org.uk.
Southwold and Walberswick (7½ and 4¼ miles) – the former is a very pretty seaside community with its own little pier (but the locals will blanch if you call the town a 'resort'); while the latter is a beautiful quiet village, made all the quieter by the second homes owned by moderately famous people. Travel between the two across the River Blyth on the Southwold–Walberswick ferry (a rowing boat); 80p per person; June to September 10am–12:30pm & 2–7pm (for non-summer timetable see website); www.explorewalberswick.co.uk/ferry.php.

open	All year
tiny campsites' rating	✹ ✹
friendliness	☺☺
cost	BP ££, Couple ££, Family ££

Potton Hall is real hidey-hole of a site. At a polite distance from the Suffolkian hotspots of Dunwich and Southwold, the site is a good quarter of a mile off the road, up a dirt track. A simple field is sheltered on three sides, while what looks like a sort of mill stream, but is actually the River Dunwich, runs down the length of it, garlanded with bulrushes. The many-gabled Potton Hall, parts of which date back to the 17th century, sits just the other side of a tall hedge. Around and

about flit nightingales, barn owls, red deer, muntjac deer, badgers and voles.

This is a rare adults-only site (see also the Little Oasis, p150 and Silver Birches, p162) and there are no loos or showers, so you'll either have to bring your own facilities or make for the wilds with a trowel and a sense of adventure. However, the owners do run a renowned recording studio on the grounds so you can bring an instrument and a wad of cash and make that album you've always threatened to unleash upon the world.

Dunwich (2¼ miles), which can be reached by footpath through Dunwich Forest, was once the second most important port in England (after London) and possessor of no fewer than 52 churches. The sea has since battered the place – one storm took 400 houses with it – so that nowadays Dunwich barely rustles up enough houses to call itself a village, while the harbour is sleepy to the point of comatose.

Grove Road
Norfolk
NR16 2HQ

📧 Mr and Mrs Greenwood
☎ 01953 887223
📧 mark.sara1@sky.com
🗺 Landranger: 144 (TM 054 880)

THE BASICS
Size: ²/₅ acre.
Pitches: Variable (0 hard standing)
Terrain: Flat.
Shelter: Some pitches.
View: Paddocks.
Waterside: No.
Electric hook-ups: 5.
Noise/Light/Olfactory pollution: No.

THE FACILITIES
Loos: 2U. **Showers**: 1U (free).
Other facilities: Indoor pool, info shed, picnic tables, CDP.
Stuff for children: Chickens, sheep, horses; swings. **Recycling**: Everything.

THE RULES
Dogs: Yes, under control. **Fires**: No open fires; BBQs off ground. **Other**: No.

PUB LIFE
The Banham Barrel, Banham Zoo (½ mile) – the closest pub, but food only served at w/e lunchtimes; open Mon–Thur 4–11pm, Fri 2pm–midnight, Sat 12–midnight, Sun till 10pm; food served w/es 12–3pm; 01953 888593; www.banhambarrel.co.uk.
For an evening meal head for the **Red Lion**, Kenninghall (2 miles) – 18th-century real-ale pub with a range of music nights; open Mon–Thur 12–3pm & 5:30–11pm, Fri–Sat 12–11pm, Sun till 10:30pm; lunch served 12–2pm, dinner Sun–Thur 7–9pm, Fri & Sat till 9:30pm; 01953 887849; www.redlionkenninghall.co.uk.

SHOP
Londis, opposite Banham Zoo (½ mile) – large convenience store with lots of locally

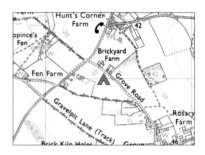

sourced products; open 7am–9pm 7D; 01953 887320.

THERE AND AWAY
Train station: Eccles Road (3½ miles) – Norwich to Ely line. Turner and Butcher run a no. 1 minibus once a day (8.55am) from Eccles Road to Banham.

OUT AND ABOUT
Banham Zoo (½ mile) – serial winner of the Best Norfolk Attraction award and committed to keeping endangered species from extinction; adult £12.95, child £8.95, U3 free; open from 10am (closing time according to season); 01953 887771; www.banhamzoo.co.uk.
Bressingham Steam and Gardens (5 miles) – ride on a steam train around gardens before visiting a recreation of *Dad's Army*'s Walmington-on-Sea – do days out get any better? Adult £9.50, child (3–16) £6.50, family £27 (including unlimited train rides); open daily (though no trains Mon–Tue) 10:30am–5pm (till 5:30pm June–August); 01379 686 900; www.bressingham.co.uk.

open	All year
tiny campsites' rating	★★★
friendliness	☺☺
cost	BP £££, Couple £££, Family £££

Ask most tourists to name anything in the area of Norfolk between Thetford in the west and Norwich in the east, and they'll scratch their heads and mumble something about Fakenham (which doesn't count as it's too far north). This 30-mile-wide stretch of apparent terra nullius is, of course, nothing of the sort – it's full of expansive swathes of greenery and interesting little villages and, better still, very few tourists.

At Brickyard Farm, the openness of the scenery and the relative lack of people in it is preserved within the campsite itself. 'Full' here means there's still plenty of room to play frisbee or a favourite ball game without endangering the lives of other campers when Uncle Brian's googly inevitably goes very wrong.

However, it's the indoor swimming pool (adult £3.50, child £2.50 per hour) that is the great draw here. Campers use the pool's shower and loo, and the smell of warm chlorine every time one passes through acts as a constant temptation to plunge in and bang out some lengths (or just to plunge in and wallow).

There are paddocks all around the camping field, where horses can often be seen grazing, exercising or doing whatever else it is horses do. Chickens roam freely, while sheep saunter about in a pen, much to the delight of any children staying on the site.

And if you do tire of this largely undiscovered part of the county, the attractions of both the north and the east coasts are within reach for day trips.

Stiffkey Road
Morston
Holt
Norfolk
NR25 7BJ

Mr E Hamond
01263 740188
ned@hamond.co.uk
www.glavenvalley.co.uk/scaldbeck
OS Landranger: 133 (TG 004 440)

THE BASICS
Size: ⅕ acre.
Pitches: Max. 12 people (0 hard standing).
Terrain: Very gently sloping.
Shelter: To east and north.
View: The field next door.
Waterside: No, but sea just 150 metres away at high tide.
Electric hook-ups: No.
Noise/Light/Olfactory pollution: During daytime some traffic on main road, 200 metres away.

THE FACILITIES
Loos: 1U. **Showers**: 1U.
Other facilities: Outdoor washing-up area, picnic tables.
Stuff for children: No.
Recycling: Everything.

THE RULES
Dogs: Yes, under control (chickens around).
Fires: Open fires allowed in designated area (must bring own wood); BBQ and breeze blocks available.
Other: Don't feed the horses.

PUB LIFE
Anchor Inn (free house), Morston (¼ mile) – highly regarded food (book ahead) if somewhat chaotic service; open Mon–Sat 11am–11pm, Sun till 10:30pm; food served Mon–Sat 12–2:30pm & 6–9pm, Sun 12–8pm; 01263 741392.

SHOP
Spar, Blakeney (1½ miles along coastal path) – large convenience store; open 8am–10pm 7D; 01263 740339.

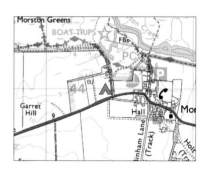

THERE AND AWAY
Train station: Sheringham (11 miles) – Sheringham to Norfolk line. The Coasthopper bus (www.coasthopper.co.uk) from Sheringham to King's Lynn stops right outside the site.

OUT AND ABOUT
Norfolk Coast Path – the 47-mile walk goes right past the campsite and takes in some of the country's most interesting coastline, from salt marshes and mudflats to cliffs (yes, in Norfolk); www.nationaltrail.co.uk/PeddarsWay.
Seal-watching boat trips from Morston Quay (¼ mile) – see the seals (and birds) on Blakeney Point; adult £8, U14 £4; daily sailings (times dependent on tide – see websites); Bean Boats 01263 740038; www.beansboattrips.co.uk; and Temple Boats 01263 740791; www.sealtrips.co.uk. The campsite owners are happy to book one for you.
Sailing School, Morston Quay (¼ mile) – various courses for children and adults; 01263 740704; www.norfolketc.co.uk.

open	Easter to October (or later, if weather permits)
tiny campsites' rating	★ ★
friendliness	☺☺☺
cost	BP ££, Couple ££, Family £££££

Travel along the main north Norfolk coast road between Sheringham and Hunstanton and, just west of the village of Morston, you'll pass a very missable hand-painted sign bearing the legend 'B&B no en suite'. This is the subtle introduction to Scaldbeck Cottage, which turns out to be a fine-looking traditional Norfolk flint cottage with a petite camping field just beyond its garden.

It's an informal affair. Access to the site is around the back of the cottage, under trees and past Marans chickens and upturned rowing boats, while a path off through the garden leads to the loo/shower. Do pop a mallet in with your luggage, because although the grass looks soft enough, the ground beneath it is really quite hard after the first inch and will take a certain delight in bending your pegs should you attempt to ram them in with your foot.

Just a five-minute stroll from bustling Morston Quay, the site is ideal for hikers who want a base from which to attempt sections of the Norfolk Coast Path. Simply take the excellent Coasthopper bus to whichever point you want to walk along, then let it bring your weary legs back in the evening.

There's a cooked breakfast available (£7) if booked the night before – either a full English ('a breakfast for kings') with a slew of home-made ingredients or a veggie alternative. In the event of fire, famine, pestilence or the sword, the cottage also has a couple of rooms on a B&B basis.

Little Thetford
Cambridgeshire
CB6 3HL

Matt Bedford
01353 662386 & 07833 391234
Landranger: 143 (TL 533 775)

THE BASICS
Size: ¼ acre.
Pitches: 4 (0 hard standing).
Terrain: Flat.
Shelter: All sides except to north
(prevailing wind is from south).
View: 2 miles across fields to Ely Cathedral.
Waterside: No.
Electric hook-ups: 4.
Noise/Light/Olfactory pollution: There's
surprisingly little noise from the road or
the trains, though that's not to say there's
none at all.

THE FACILITIES
Loos: 1U. **Showers**: No.
Other facilities: CDP.
Stuff for children: No.
Recycling: Everything.

THE RULES
Dogs: Under control.
Fires: No open fires; BBQs off grass.
Other: In winter only tents and caravans
towed by 4WD vehicles are permitted.

PUB LIFE
The Cutter Inn (independent), Ely (2 miles)
– this pub/restaurant right on the river has
only been open since 2006 but is already
a multi-award-winner (and does a gluten-
free menu too); open 12–9pm 7D; food
served throughout the day; 01353 662713;
www.thecutterinn.co.uk.

SHOP
Budgens, Witchford Road roundabout,
A10/A142, Ely (1½ miles) – a convenience
store at a petrol station – not the loveliest
of places in the world to visit but useful in

an emergency; open 5am–11pm 7D;
01353 669112.

THERE AND AWAY
Train station: Ely (2 miles) – Cambridge to
King's Lynn line. From Ely, the Stagecoach
(www.stagecoachbus.com) bus no. X9
passes the farm.

OUT AND ABOUT
Ely Cathedral (2¼ miles) – having seen it
from afar, you might as well have a look
at what's inside; adult £5.50, child £4.70
(including guided tour); open daily in
summer 7am–7pm; 01353 667735;
www.elycathedral.org.
Wicken Fen, Wicken (7 miles) – various
trails on the National Trust's oldest nature
reserve carry visitors over a wetland area
brimming with rare species of wildlife
(and there's a café too); adult £5, child
£2.50, family £12.70; open daily April to
November 10am–5pm (in other months
sometimes closed on Mon); 01353 720274;
www.wicken.org.uk.

open	All year
tiny campsites' rating	★★
friendliness	☺☺
cost	BP £, Couple ££, Family ££

Braham Farm delights far beyond expectation. Look at the map and the signs are not hopeful: there's a railway line to one side and the main Ely to Cambridge road on the other. However, once you've left the frenzied race track of the A10 behind you and have made your way across a field to the farmhouse, a much more promising picture emerges.

Around the side of a wonderful old farmhouse there's a large lawn with a simply fantastic view across wheat fields to Ely Cathedral. At this point you could be forgiven for continuing your search for the campsite in some field beyond, but the joyful truth is that the large lawn is the campsite and the wonderful old farmhouse its perfect backdrop.

But back to the view. Somehow, rather than glimpsing just the very tips of the towers of the elegant house of worship, whole swathes of what travel writer HV Morton once described as 'the only feminine cathedral in England' are visible. If you care to walk to it (it's only a couple of miles away), a footpath from the farm takes you to within a stone's throw (though best not, with all that stained glass about).

Cross another part of this 450-acre arable farm and dive under the railway line, and you can join the 150-mile Ouse Valley Way (www.ousevalleyway.org.uk), or the more modest 50-mile Fen Rivers Way (tinyurl.com/y9aoaxa) as they surge along the banks of the River Great Ouse.

Central England

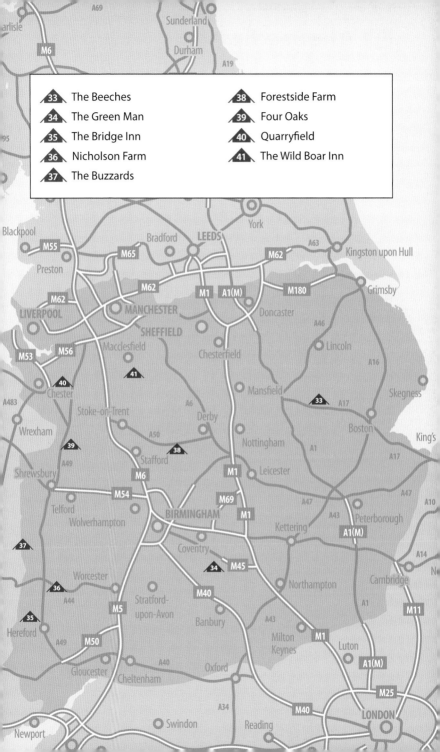

Legend:

- 33 — The Beeches
- 34 — The Green Man
- 35 — The Bridge Inn
- 36 — Nicholson Farm
- 37 — The Buzzards
- 38 — Forestside Farm
- 39 — Four Oaks
- 40 — Quarryfield
- 41 — The Wild Boar Inn

33 The Beeches

Byard's Leap
Cranwell
Lincolnshire
NG34 8EY

Mike and Paula Cooper
01400 262637
mentalmicky2@btinternet.com
www.bubblecarmuseum.co.uk
OS Landranger: 130 (SK 989 494)

THE BASICS
Size: ½ acre.
Pitches: Variable (0 hard standing).
Terrain: Flat.
Shelter: Yes.
View: No.
Waterside: No.
Electric hook-ups: 6.
Noise/Light/Olfactory pollution: Traffic on A17; occasional light planes from nearby airfield.

THE FACILITIES
Loos: 2M 2W. **Showers**: 1M 1W (10p for '1 min' – takes 10p, 20p & £1 coins).
Other facilities: CDP.
Stuff for children: Museum, adventure playground.
Recycling: Everything.

THE RULES
Dogs: On leads.
Fires: No open fires; BBQs off grass.
Other: No.

PUB LIFE
The George Hotel, Leadenham (3¼ miles) – a historic and handsome coaching inn with a separate restaurant and the second largest collection of whiskies in Britain; open 11:45am–3pm & 5:45pm–midnight 7D; food served 12–2pm & 6–9pm 7D (Sat till 9:30pm); 01400 272251.

SHOP
Spar/NAAFI, RAF Cranwell (1 mile) – goods store; open Mon–Fri 7am–10pm, w/es 9am–10pm; 01400 261332.

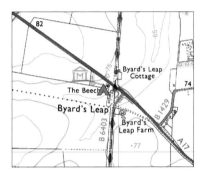

THERE AND AWAY
Train station: Ancaster (3 miles) – Nottingham to Skegness line. No onward bus service to the site.

OUT AND ABOUT
Bubble Car Museum (on site) – now also offering 10-minute rides around the countryside in a Heinkel/Trojan, Messerschmitt or Bond Bug on selected dates; museum entrance adult £2.50, child 75p; open end May to November Sat/Sun/BH 10am–4pm (also open Fri in July and August).
Belton House, Belton, nr Grantham (9 miles) – as seen in productions of *Jane Eyre*, *Pride and Prejudice* and *Tom Jones*, the 17th-century country house enjoys some astutely laid-out gardens and a swathe of parkland; adult £9.09, child £5.45, family £24.09; open mid March to October Wed–Sun 11am–5pm; 01476 566116; NT site. Or nose around the similarly decorous village for free.

open	All year
tiny campsites' rating	✷✷
friendliness	☺☺
cost	BP £, Couple ££, Family ££

Not an elegant site exactly, but the Beeches does score points for sheer quirkiness for the 40-foot-long narrowboat up on stilts in one corner.

More conventionally, another corner is given over to a small copse, mainly of old hawthorns, in which campers are allowed, indeed encouraged, to pitch among the trees 'alongside the rabbits'. Since this is Lincolnshire, a county in which the wind has never been known to drop below 50 knots for more than 30 seconds at a time, any shelter is to be welcomed, although you should beware of the baby stinging nettles poking up through the undergrowth as you stick your pegs into the pleasingly friable, paw-churned topsoil.

The great draw here is the Bubble Car Museum. Opened in 2003 to house Mike's personal collection, it's crammed with, well, bubble cars; although the refreshingly dangerous-looking micro three-wheelers also come in many shapes other than bubble. The famous orange Bond Bug is here, as is a monstrous bulbous affair called Bamby that one can't help feeling should have been shot along with its mother, as well as a wonderful wooden caravan from the 1950s that is little more than a Wendy house on wheels. There's also a small café and a side collection of everyday ephemera from the last century, which has every visitor over 40 pointing excitedly and declaring to anyone who will listen that, 'Yes, we had one of those – exactly the same, I tell you.'

There are three picnic tables on the site, while loos and showers are in a small well-maintained pavilion.

Church Road
Long Itchington
Warwickshire
CV47 9PW

Mark Carver-Smith
01926 812208
greenmanlongitch@aol.com
Landranger: 151 (SP 410 651)

THE BASICS
Size: ½ acre.
Pitches: 10 (1 hard standing).
Terrain: Flat.
Shelter: Yes.
View: No.
Waterside: Yes, River Itchen.
Electric hook-ups: No.
Noise/Light/Olfactory pollution: No.

THE FACILITIES
Loos: 2M 2W (open from 7:30am to pub closing time). **Showers**: No.
Other facilities: CDP, picnic tables; campers can also use the kitchen to wash-up.
Stuff for children: No.
Recycling: No.

THE RULES
Dogs: On leads at all times.
Fires: No open fires; blocks available for BBQs. **Other**: No.

PUB LIFE
The Green Man (independent) –
open Mon–Fri 5pm–midnight, w/es
12–midnight. Sadly, they don't serve
food, but all five other pubs in the village
– the **Buck and Bell** (01926 811177), the
Cuttle Inn (01926 812314), the **Harvester**
(happily, not *a* Harvester; 01926 812698),
Duck on the Pond (01926 815876) and
the **Two Boats Inn** (01926 812640) – do.

SHOP
Co-op Lateshop, Long Itchington
(150 metres) – mini supermarket; open
Mon–Sat 7am–8pm, Sun till 4pm;
01926 812411.

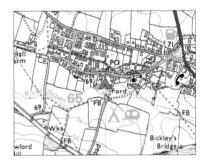

THERE AND AWAY
Train station: Leamington Spa (6½
miles) – London to Birmingham line.
Stagecoach's bus no. 64 from Leamington
Spa stops right outside the pub.

OUT AND ABOUT
Heritage Motor Centre, Gaydon (10 miles)
– a collection huge enough to satisfy even
the most ardent of petrolheads; adult £9,
child (5–16) £7, U5 free, family £28; open
daily all year 10am–5pm; 01926 641188.
Boating, Leamington Spa (6 miles) – hire
a motor boat, rowing skiff, canoe, kayak or
pedalo, and take off down the River Leam;
from £9/hour; open daily June to August
and at w/es the rest of the year; 01926
889928; www.leamboatcentre.com.
Leamington Spa Art Gallery & Museum
(6½ miles) – LS Lowry, Marc Quinn, Stanley
Spencer, Gillian Wearing and more, in the
former hydrotherapy pool at the Royal
Pump Rooms; free; open Tue/Wed/Fri/Sat
10:30am–5pm, Thur 1:30–8pm, Sun/BH
11am–4pm; 01926 742700;
tinyurl.com/dj7r3y.

open	All year
tiny campsites' rating	★ ★
friendliness	☺☺☺
cost	BP ££, Couple ££, Family ££

Some pub campsites can be very disappointing: even if the pub itself is lovely, the portion allotted for camping is all too often an unloved crisp-packet-strewn patch of ground. Not so at the Green Man, where, over the last few years, landlord Mark has transformed the tatty green he inherited when he took over the pub. What once was only suitable for holding the annual village bonfire is now a beautiful little patch of countryside. Damsons and an enormous old plum tree circle a picnic table, itself tucked into a little dell beneath which runs a narrow and incredibly lazy stretch of the River Itchen. There's a miniature woodland walk through the trees and each spring a figure of eight course is mown through the high cow parsley. Meanwhile, free-range hens of every hue and shade scratch and strut their way between the tents.

Long Itchington is the self-styled Real Ale Capital of England and it's a claim that is difficult to dispute. It has six pubs, which for a pretty standard-size village is a remarkable feat in itself, and half of them (the Green Man included) feature in the *Good Beer Guide*, while the other three also serve real ale.

There's no food at the Green Man, but a fish-and-chip van stops outside the pub on Friday nights at 7:30pm and comes highly recommended. Furthermore, all five other pubs in the village serve food and are only a short stagger away.

The Bridge Inn

Michaelchurch Escley
Herefordshire
HR2 0JW

Nick and Karen Maddy
01981 510646
nickmaddy@aol.com
Landranger: 161 (SO 317 341)

THE BASICS
Size: ³/₅ acre.
Pitches: 15 (3 hard standing).
Terrain: Flat.
Shelter: Yes.
View: No.
Waterside: Yes, the Escley brook.
Electric hook-ups: 6.
Noise/Light/Olfactory pollution: Only whatever noise emanates from the pub or the car park, and it's possible to nab a pitch away from both.

THE FACILITIES
Loos: 2M 2W. **Showers**: 1M 1W (free).
Other facilities: Belfast sink in ladies'.
Stuff for children: Children's playground, various toys, swings in trees.
Recycling: Bottles, shoes (oh yes).

THE RULES
Dogs: On leads.
Fires: BBQs; fires off the ground.
Other: No parking on the grass.

PUB LIFE
The Bridge Inn (free house; on the doorstep) – open Mon–Fri 12–3pm & 6pm–'late', w/es 12–'late'; food served Mon–Fri 12–3pm & 6–9pm, w/es 12–9pm.

SHOP
Hopes of Longtown, (3½ miles) – a stylish curving roof on a modern wooden building that houses a comprehensive range of victuals and an off licence; open Mon/Tue/Wed/Fri 8:30am–5:30pm, Thur till 8pm, Sat till 4pm, open Sun from April to October 10am–2pm; 01873 860444; www.hopesoflongtown.co.uk.

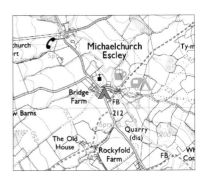

THERE AND AWAY
Train station: Abergavenny (14 miles) or Hereford (15 miles) – Shrewsbury to Newport line. From Abergavenny, walk to nearby Llanfoist Fawr, take bus no. X4 (www.stagecoachbus.com) to Pontrilas and pick up the Nick Maddy Coaches' no. 440 to Michaelchurch Escley.

OUT AND ABOUT
The 177-mile **Offa's Dyke Path** (www.nationaltrail.co.uk/offasdyke) and the **Black Mountains** (tinyurl.com/yaohsrl) are just 4 miles away as the crow flies (though the crow will need to gain some height); both offer superb walking possibilities.
Llanthony (13½ miles by road, around 5 by footpath) – a hamlet in the high Vale of Ewyas that plays host to the ruins of 12th-century Llanthony Priory, part of which is an exquisite hotel whose bar is always worth a visit (hours depend on season; 01873 890487; www.llanthonyprioryhotel.co.uk).

open	All year
tiny campsites' rating	★ ★
friendliness	☺
cost	BP £, Couple ££, Family £££

There's a small back road from the Welsh village of Pandy that skirts around the bottom of the Black Mountains, and so unwittingly finds itself in England for a stretch. Just before it heads back for the border at Hay-on-Wye, it slides into Michaelchurch Escley, a sinuous village named after both its church and its brook. At one of the few turnings-off sits the deftliest of hidden pubs, the Bridge Inn.

The demarcation here is clear: campervans and caravans are corralled by the riverside, while a grassy terrace plays host to the two-man tents. The top terrace – a sunny circle bounded by trees – accommodates the family-sized dwellings. In summer, children play in the stream by the inn's eponymous bridge, while their parents sit out in the beer garden pretending to keep an eye on them. The pub, a low-beamed inn of indeterminate age, was once a place where drovers slaked their thirst before taking their herds or flocks across the river. Today it still serves locally brewed real ales and meals that use locally sourced produce wherever possible.

A large folder in the pub bulges with scores of local walks – if you did one a day you'd be here all summer – urging hikers up to Hergest Ridge, the Devil's Pulpit, Arthur's Stone and beyond. The cycling is pretty good here too, with plenty of very minor roads wending their way from somnolent village to somnolent village, before surprising the patient pedaller with huge open vistas of the Herefordshire hills.

Docklow
Leominster
Herefordshire
HR6 0SL

Tim Brooke
07740 717564
tjwbrooke@aol.com
www.nicholsonfarm.co.uk
OS Landranger: 149 (SO 584 580)

THE BASICS
Size: 1 acre.
Pitches: 10 (3 hard standing).
Terrain: Mainly flat.
Shelter: To west.
View: East to Herefordshire farm.
Waterside: No, but there's a lake in the valley below.
Electric hook-ups: 10.
Noise/Light/Olfactory pollution: No.

THE FACILITIES
Loos: 2W 2M. **Showers**: 1W 1M (free and excellent).
Other facilities: Microwave, double Belfast sink for washing-up, CDP.
Stuff for children: 3 swings.
Recycling: Glass, food stuffs.

THE RULES
Dogs: If well behaved.
Fires: No open fires; BBQs off ground (BBQ available on site).
Other: No large groups.

PUB LIFE
King's Head (free house), Docklow (2 miles) – recently taken over by a trained chef and her husband; the campsite owner will ferry people here by arrangement; open 12–3pm & 6pm –'when everyone leaves' 7D; food served 12–2pm & 6–9pm 7D; 01568 760560.

SHOP
Co-op, Bromyard (5¼ miles) – small supermarket; open Mon–Sat 8am–10pm, Sun 10am–4pm; 01885 488808.

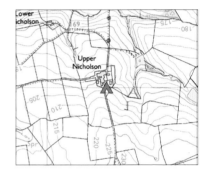

THERE AND AWAY
Train station: Leominster (6 miles) – Shrewsbury to Hereford line. No onward bus to site.

OUT AND ABOUT
Stockton Bury Gardens, Kimbolton (6 miles) – a 4-acre garden with many rare and interesting plants set among medieval buildings including a tithe barn (which is also a restaurant), grotto, cider press and 'a mock ruined chapel'; 01568 613432; www.stocktonbury.co.uk.
Brockhampton Estate (7¼ miles) – signed walks through parkland and woodland rich in wildlife, with wooden sculptures scattered throughout; £2.60pp; open daily from dawn to dusk; 01885 488099; NT site. There's also a medieval manor on the estate – see website for the complex opening times and prices.

open	Easter to October
tiny campsites' rating	★★
friendliness	☺☺☺
cost	BP ££, Couple ££, Family £££

Goshawks, sparrowhawks, kestrels and all manner of owls have made themselves at home on Nicholson Farm, taking advantage of its lofty position in the north Herefordshire hills. Buzzards, meanwhile, are practically as common as blackbirds, and your chances of staying here and not seeing one are slim indeed.

Even when the air is not filled with predatory birds, the view from this family-orientated campsite is a very pleasant one, taking in the surrounding hills, many of which form part of this 200-acre dairy farm. The owner, Tim, will give visitors a tour on request, and children may even lend a small helping hand if they ask really nicely.

The campsite, which is located beside the 17th-century farmhouse, is a good quarter of a mile from the main road and down a little dip, so is blissfully shielded from any traffic noise. At the foot of the valley below the site there's a lake heaving with fish of all sizes: fishing permits can be bought from the farm.

Bicycle hire can also be arranged on site. The extremely visitable towns of Leominster, Bromyard and Tenbury Wells are equidistant from the farm and well within two-wheel striking range for even the rustiest of cyclists.

There's also B&B to be had at the farmhouse – including one room with a gargantuan four-poster bed – in case any members of your party are not natural campers. Trivia fans, meanwhile, will be excited to learn that much of the farm's milk is sent away to become Cadbury's Dairy Milk chocolate.

Kingsland
Leominster
Herefordshire
HR6 9QE

Elaine Povey
01568 708941
holiday@thebuzzards.co.uk
www.thebuzzards.co.uk
Landranger: 148 (SO 420 629)

THE BASICS
Size: ¼ acre.
Pitches: 20 (2 hard standing).
Terrain: Flat.
Shelter: Yes.
View: Hill.
Waterside: Yes, a small pond.
Electric hook-ups: No.
Noise/Light/Olfactory pollution: No.

THE FACILITIES
Loos: 1U. **Showers**: 1U (free).
Other facilities: Washing-up sink, fridge/freezer, free-range eggs and other organic home-grown produce for sale including meat, tomatoes, salads, plums and apples.
Stuff for children: Animals (with parental supervision).
Recycling: Everything (inc. compost).

THE RULES
Dogs: On leads.
Fires: Open fires in specified areas; BBQs off ground. **Other**: No.

PUB LIFE
Mortimers Cross Inn (¾ mile) – a pub dating back to the 12th century (check out the inglenook and the well in the restaurant) and run by a young couple who like a good party and locally sourced food; open Mon 4:30–11pm, Tue–Fri 12–2:30pm & 4:30–11pm, Sat 12–11pm, Sun till 10:30pm; food served Mon 7–9pm, Tue–Sat 12–2pm & 7–9pm, Sun 12–2pm; 01568 709212; www.mortimerscrossinn.com.

SHOP
The Village Green PO (and coffee shop), Kingsland (2½ miles) – basics plus a tiny deli

and a small off licence with an emphasis on locally produced food and drink; Mon–Tue & Thur–Fri 8:30am–5:30pm, Wed till 2pm, Sat till 1pm (coffee shop open Mon–Sat 10am–4:30pm); 01568 708201. There are also community-run stores at Yarpole (3 miles) and Wigmore (3½ miles).

THERE AND AWAY
Train station: Leominster (7 miles) – Shrewsbury to Hereford line. Owner can collect/drop off at Leominster station by prior arrangement.

OUT AND ABOUT
Berrington Hall, nr Leominster (8 miles) – neoclassical mansion in landscaped grounds; adult £6.15, child £3.05, family £15.45; house open March to November Sat–Wed 1–5pm; 01568 615721; NT site.
Black and White Trail, Kingsland (2½ miles) is the closest port of call for this 40-mile circular trip around Herefordshire's black and white timber-framed houses; tinyurl.com/ybby3qb.

open	All year
tiny campsites' rating	★★★
friendliness	☺☺☺
cost	BP £££, Couple £££, Family £££

Once you've arrived at the Buzzards, the difficulty is deciding where to go first. The badger hide, perhaps? Or the bluebell-carpeted wood for some bat-watching? Or maybe a visit to scratch the ears of Barbara, the big Tamworth sow?

It's hard to believe that this biodynamic smallholding only covers 16 acres, so packed is it with happy diversions. The delights continue at the secluded campsite, which enjoys a private view up the wooded valley. The loo/shower, meanwhile, is attached to the main house, a short step away.

Should you care to wander, this part of Herefordshire is packed with things to see and do including Croft Castle (3 miles; 01568 780141; NT site), the 30-mile Mortimer Trail (Aymestry, 1¼ miles; tinyurl.com/y9wffdb) and the Dunkerton's cider orchards and chocolaterie (6¼ miles; 01544 388161; www.dunkertons.co.uk), while each village in the area has its own short circular walks (leaflets available on site).

A good many people, however, simply prefer to take root in the camping field, enjoying the visits from the three friendly cats; ruffling the coats of the two hand-reared sheep; ambling along to the mere by the woods to commune with the grebes, coots and moorhens; or merely chatting with Elaine, owner of the Buzzards and the very soul of kindness.

For 2010, there's the promise of an even more secluded space for those who seriously want to get away from it all: a separate pitch in the small ancient quarry from which the stone came to build the farmhouse.

Marchington Cliff
Uttoxeter
Staffordshire
ST14 8NA

Chris and Janette Prince
01283 820353
stay@forestsidefarm.co.uk
www.forestsidefarm.co.uk
Landranger: 128 (SK 132 291)

THE BASICS
Size: 1 acre.
Pitches: 17 – max. 30 people (5 hard standing).
Terrain: Gently sloping.
Shelter: Trees to south.
View: North towards Peak District.
Waterside: No.
Electric hook-ups: 8.
Noise/Light/Olfactory pollution: The occasional nocturnal roar of a cow validating its existence in the field next door.

THE FACILITIES
Loos: 2M 2W. **Showers**: 2M 2W (free).
Other facilities: Washing-up area, fridge, kettle, microwave, tourist information, coarse fishing passes, CDP.
Stuff for children: Kids can watch the cows being milked if under supervision.
Recycling: Everything.

THE RULES
Dogs: On leads at all times. **Fires**: No open fires; BBQs off grass. **Other**: No.

PUB LIFE
The Roebuck Inn (Marston's), Draycott in the Clay (2½ miles); open 12–11pm 7D; food served Mon–Sat 12–3pm & 6–9pm, Sun 12–3pm; 01283 820973.
In the absence of easily walkable food-serving pubs, you could try **The Barn** (1 mile), an Indian restaurant on the road towards Draycott in the Clay; 01283 820367.

SHOP
Marchington Village Shop (1 mile) – basics and newspapers; Mon–Fri 8am–6pm, w/es 8:30am–noon; 01283 821248.

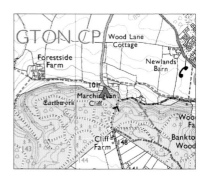

THERE AND AWAY
Train station: Uttoxeter (5¼ miles) – Derby to Crewe line. The Arriva Midlands North (www.arrivabus.co.uk) bus no. 402 runs from Uttoxeter train station to Marchington Cliff.

OUT AND ABOUT
Sudbury Hall & Museum of Childhood, Sudbury (4¾ miles) – a grand 17th-century mansion, a childhood museum and host of frequent special events; joint entry to mansion and museum: adult £12, child £6.36, family £30.36 (further reduction if arriving by bicycle or public transport); open on varying days according to season from mid February to mid December; 01283 585305; NT site.
Tutbury Castle (6¼ miles) – a prison for Mary Queen of Scots and biffed about by the Roundheads: plenty of history to get your teeth into; adult £4.50, child (5–12) £4, U5 free, family £14; open all year Wed–Sun 11am–5pm; 01283 812129; www.tutburycastle.com.

open	All year
tiny campsites' rating	★★
friendliness	☺☺☺
cost	BP £££, Couple ££££, Family £££££

There are some campsites that merely aspire to views and others that have them in spades. Look north from Forestside, a 156-acre organic dairy farm, and you'll enjoy a 180-degree vista that takes in both the Weaver Hills and the Peak District's Dove Valley, and still has room for more around the edges. At night, all those distant parts that looked uninhabited suddenly switch on their lights, presumably for the benefit of those watching from the farm.

The site consists of an upper mown field with a slightly rougher field below for those who prefer their camping a little less refined. As the name suggests, the farm is right next to a wood (listen out for tawny owls in the evening) that rises steeply behind it up Marchington Cliff, giving some shelter to the south. A sort of very upmarket shed houses the facilities including four highly civilised shower rooms. In the tourist info room there are some laminated maps of a short, circular farm walk to sharpen your appetite for dinner or get the blood circulating in the morning.

Here, your most difficult decision is where you spend the rest of your day, as there are numerous attractions within striking distance to tempt you off the premises (see also facing page), including horse racing at Uttoxeter (4¾ miles) to the heart-stoppingly beautiful Manifold Valley cycle trail (18 miles; tinyurl.com/y8hw9r2). Don't mention it to the kids, but you're also just a dozen miles from Alton Towers.

Lower House Farm
Whixall
Shropshire
SY13 2NG

Mr Williams
01948 880241
OS Landranger: 126 (SJ 522 348)

THE BASICS
Size: ²/₃ acre.
Pitches: Variable (0 hard standing).
Terrain: Flat.
Shelter: All round.
View: Into next field.
Waterside: Yes, a large pond.
Electric hook-ups: No.
Noise/Light/Olfactory pollution: No.

THE FACILITIES
Loos (open air): 1U. **Showers**: No.
Other facilities: No.
Stuff for children: No. **Recycling**: No.

THE RULES
Dogs: Yes. **Fires**: Open fires; BBQs off grass.
Other: No.

PUB LIFE
Bull and Dog (free house), Coton
(1¾ miles) – the *Shropshire Star* gave
the food here 4 stars, and we know
they wouldn't lie to us; open Mon–Fri
12–2:30pm & 5–11pm, Sat 12–11pm,
Sun till 10:30pm; food served Mon–Fri
12–2:30pm & 5:30–9pm (Fri till 9:30pm),
Sat 12–9:30pm, Sun till 8pm;
01948 880559.

SHOP
Coton Oaks, Coton (3 miles) – a farm shop
and café with Internet facilities; stocks a
few basics, some deli goodies, plus wine
and local beers; open Mon–Fri 8am–5pm,
Sat till 4pm; 01948 840592.

THERE AND AWAY
Train station: Prees (3 miles) – a request
stop on the Shrewsbury to Crewe line. No

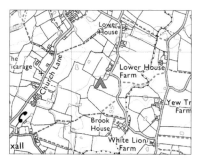

direct bus service to the site, so hop in a
taxi for the rest of the journey.

OUT AND ABOUT
Hawkstone Follies (6½ miles) – a
200-year-old fantasia of weird and
wonderful monuments in a land of caves,
crags and woods; adult £6, child £4, family
£17; open daily from late May to August,
10am–3:30pm (for non-summer opening
times see website); 01948 841700;
tinyurl.com/nxhtce.
Whixall Moss (2 miles) – a nature reserve
so large it's visible from space (guided
walks also available); 01948 880362.
The market towns of **Wem** (4¼ miles) and
Whitchurch (5 miles) are also worth a
mosey around.

open	All year
tiny campsites' rating	★★
friendliness	☺☺
cost	BP £, Couple £, Family £

If any site exemplified the concept of 'hideaway' it's this one. First you must find Lower House Farm, which is tucked away within a maze of tiny roads. Then, rather than calling in at the farmhouse, you should proceed to the brand new dwelling immediately to its left. From here you will be directed on an almost circular tour of yet more minor roads for the best part of a mile, arriving eventually at an unmarked gate in a hedge. Pass through this, across a field and through another gate and you're there.

Congratulations. Plans are afoot to construct a track across the fields to link the site to the new house at Lower House Farm, but until then the getting there only increases the anticipation and is all part of the holiday fun.

The rewards for those who make it are great. About a third of the field is given over to a large pond encircled by trees, topped with lily pads and bristling with water-loving plants. The pond is vaguely Pac-Man shaped (by chance rather than design, apparently), so if you pop your tent into the bit where the mouth would be, you're in just about the snuggest camping pitch in the country: perfect for dropping anchor and lazily observing whatever passing wildlife visits the pond.

Despite its remote location, there is not only a water tap here but a loo too. The latter is surrounded by a low wooden slatted fence, which is open to the elements but, hey, it flushes (though do remember to take your own loo paper).

Quarryfield Camping
Rode Street
Tarporley
Cheshire
CW6 0EF

Deborah and Ellis
07720 664106
ellis@quarryfieldcamping.co.uk
www.quarryfieldcamping.co.uk
Landranger: 117 (SJ 546 633)

THE BASICS
Size: ³⁄₅ acre.
Pitches: 20 (0 hard standing).
Terrain: Flat.
Shelter: All except the western side.
View: Just about – towards Chester.
Waterside: A very small (fenced off) pond.
Electric hook-ups: No.
Noise/Light/Olfactory pollution: Traffic noise from road.

THE FACILITIES
Loos: 1M 1W. **Showers**: 1U (honesty box: 25p/50p for 'short/long shower').
Other facilities: Love seat, ball games, books, washing-up area, CDP.
Stuff for children: A very tiny slide for very tiny tots.
Recycling: Everything.

THE RULES
Dogs: Under control and must be exercised off site.
Fires: No open fires; BBQs off ground.
Other: No.

PUB LIFE
The Rising Sun (free house), Tarporley (³⁄₄ mile) – low beamed and phenomenally popular; open Mon–Fri 11:30am–3pm & 5:30–11pm, Sat 11:30am–11pm, Sun 12–11pm; food served Mon–Fri 11:30am–2pm & 5:30–9:30pm, Sat 11:30am–9:30pm, Sun 12–8pm; 01829 732423.

SHOP
Co-op, Tarporley (³⁄₄ mile) – small supermarket; open 6am–10pm 7D; 01829 732498.

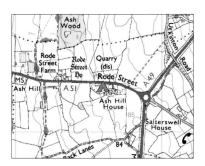

THERE AND AWAY
Train station: Delamere (5³⁄₄ miles) – a request stop on the Stockport to Chester line. From Chester the Arriva (www.arrivabus.co.uk) bus no. 84 runs past the site.

OUT AND ABOUT
Chester (10 miles) – a cathedral, a fantastic walkway around the city walls, a medieval shopping arcade and a racecourse that was once a Roman harbour; 01244 405600; www.visitchester.com.
Sandstone Trail (¼ mile) – a 34-mile north-to-south wander across rural Cheshire and north Shropshire from Frodsham to Whitchurch; www.sandstonetrail.co.uk.
Cotebrook Shirehorse Centre (2¼ miles) – 'home of the top show horses in the country' (remember your sugar lumps and they'll be eating out of the palm of your hand); adult £6.95, child £4.95, U5 free, family £10; open daily 10am–5pm (last entry 4pm); 01829 760506; www.cotebrookshirehorses.co.uk.

open	March to October
tiny campsites' rating	★ ★
friendliness	☺☺
cost	BP ££, Couple ££, Family ££

This is almost certainly the only campsite in Britain located entirely within a red sandstone quarry. The stone has long since gone, and no one is quite sure when the last quarryman upped and left but, judging by the height of the trees that have reclaimed the area, it was some considerable time ago.

At the far end there's an unobtrusive modern building incorporating two loos and a shower – all very pleasant to use – and a shelf of books you can borrow should your companions fail to entertain you adequately.

Although officially there are 20 pitches here, the owners declare it full when about half of those are taken 'so that people have room to play ball games', which does seem to be in the spirit of things. If you haven't brought your own ball with you, don't despair, because next to the washing-up area there's a stash for visitors' use.

The appealing village of Tarporley with its smattering of restaurants and pubs is less than a mile away, making it an attractive option for an evening's wander, while it would be rude to stay in a sandstone quarry and not attempt at least a little of the Sandstone Trail that runs very close by.

It's just a shame that the site is on a busy main road to Chester, because the passing cars, although out of sight, do rather dissipate the feeling of getting away from it all. However, the volume of traffic does abate as night draws on.

41 The Wild Boar Inn

Wincle
Macclesfield
Cheshire
SK11 0QL

Val Bailey and Alan Critchlow
01260 227219
www.thewildboar.co.uk
Landranger: 118 (SJ 959 671)

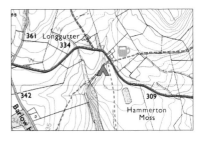

THE BASICS
Size: ⅖ acre.
Pitches: 26 (5 hard standing).
Terrain: Flat/gently sloping.
Shelter: Room for a couple of tents to hide behind trees.
View: Peak District and Cheshire hills.
Waterside: No.
Electric hook-ups: 4.
Noise/Light/Olfactory pollution: Occasional traffic.

THE FACILITIES
Loos: 2M 3W. **Showers**: 1U 1M (£1 for '5 min.'). **Other facilities**: Outdoor washing-up area, picnic tables, CDP.
Stuff for children: No.
Recycling: No.

THE RULES
Dogs: On leads at all times.
Fires: No open fires; BBQs off ground.
Other: The site is 'adult-orientated', but if you do bring kids please supervise.

PUB LIFE
The Wild Boar Inn (Robinson's; 20 metres) – open Mon–Fri at 4:30pm, Sat at noon & Sun at 11am closing 'late' every day; food served Fri 5–8:30pm, Sat 12–8:30pm, Sun till 8pm; 01260 227219.
For food Tue–Thur, try the **Crag** at Dane in Wildboarclough (pronounced 'Wilbercluff'); open Tue–Sun 11am–3pm & 7–11pm; food served Tue–Sat 12–2pm & 7–9pm, Sun 12–2pm; 01260 227239.

SHOP
Sutton PO, nr Macclesfield (3 miles) – convenience store and off licence; open

Mon–Fri 6am–7pm, Sat till 5pm, Sun till 1pm; 01260 252438. Outside these hours, there are plenty of shops in Macclesfield.

THERE AND AWAY
Train station: Macclesfield (5½ miles) – Manchester to Stoke-on-Trent line. No onward bus service to the site.

OUT AND ABOUT
Capesthorne Hall, Siddington (11¼ miles) – a Jacobean-style house filled with artworks, plus a Georgian chapel, gardens and lakes in 100 acres of parkland; hugely complex pricing system: see website and weep; open April to October Sun–Mon & BH 1:30–4pm (last admission 3:30pm); 01625 861221; www.capesthorne.com.
Lyme Park, Disley (15 miles) – a former Tudor house transformed into an Italianate palace from whose lake a certain Mr Darcy/Colin Firth emerged wet and ruffled around the edges to send a million hearts aflutter; house and garden entry: adult £7.20, child £3.60, family £18; open mid March to October Fri–Tue 11am–5pm; 01663 762023; NT site.

open	All year
tiny campsites' rating	★ ★
friendliness	☺☺
cost	BP ££, Couple £££, Family ££££

The Wild Boar Inn is many people's idea of camping heaven. Not only are there astonishing views to wake up to in the morning, at night you can step out of the pub and straight into your sleeping bag. It's a proper pub too, with copper bed-warming pans on the walls and a feeling that if you're inside when it starts snowing you could be holed up for the winter (in reality, this is a somewhat rare event).

High up on a pass between Congleton and Buxton, and remote enough not to enjoy mains water (the pub has its own bore hole), the Wild Boar is a magnet for hikers keen to walk the Dane Valley or the Staffordshire Moorlands, and for less-energetic types who simply want to spend a day or two breathing in fresh hilltop air and gazing into the distance. The pub's very reasonably priced all-day breakfasts are popular with campers and caravanners alike, who can also enjoy live music every Saturday night throughout the summer months.

Unlike the majority of pubs, the Wild Boar has its very own clay pigeon shooting team that meets every other Sunday morning around 9ish. If you're a clay pigeon shooter yourself, or just fancy shouting 'pull' before blasting away at thin air, ring Mr Roberts, the club secretary, in advance and he'll do his best to fit you in (01625 614603).

Finally, if you come to the Wild Boar by train do check out Macclesfield station's perversely brilliant platform 0.

Northern England

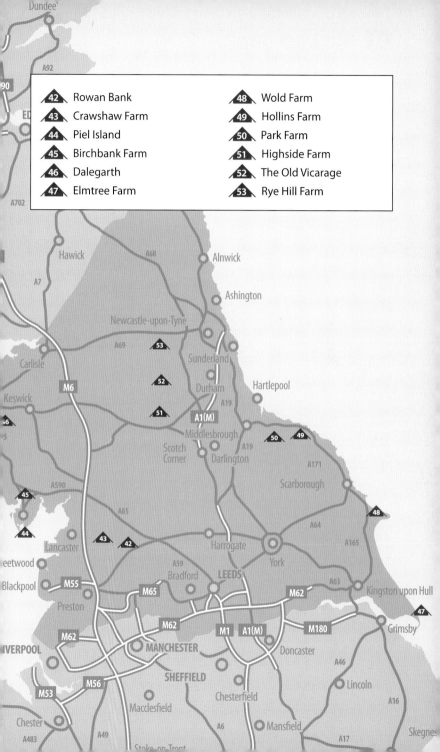

42	Rowan Bank	48	Wold Farm
43	Crawshaw Farm	49	Hollins Farm
44	Piel Island	50	Park Farm
45	Birchbank Farm	51	Highside Farm
46	Dalegarth	52	The Old Vicarage
47	Elmtree Farm	53	Rye Hill Farm

Rowan Bank

Horton in Craven
Skipton
Yorkshire
BD23 3JP

Mr AC Bancroft
01200 445291 & 07866 050845
Landranger: 103 (SD 873 503)

THE BASICS
Size: ½ acre.
Pitches: Variable (1 hard standing).
Terrain: Mainly flat.
Shelter: No.
View: A spectacular range of hills and a small town.
Waterside: No.
Electric hook-ups: 6.
Noise/Light/Olfactory pollution: Some traffic on the A59.

THE FACILITIES
Loos: No.
Showers: No.
Other facilities: CDP.
Stuff for children: No.
Recycling: Everything.

THE RULES
Dogs: Welcome – there's a playing field for them and dog-waste bins are provided.
Fires: BBQs well off grass.
Other: No.

PUB LIFE
Cross Keys (free house), East Marton (2½ miles) – a snug cottage-like pub near the Leeds and Liverpool Canal; open 11am–11pm 7D; food served Mon–Fri 12–2:30pm & 5–8:30pm, Sat 12–9pm, Sun till 8pm; 01282 844326.
White Bull (Scottish and Newcastle), Gisburn (3 miles) – a very varied menu including a range of vegetarian options; open 12–11pm 7D; food served Mon–Thur 12–2:30pm & 5:30–8:45pm, Fri–Sat all day, Sun till 7pm; 01200 445575; thewhitebullhotel.co.uk.

SHOP
The village shop at West Marton (1½ miles) was up for sale when we went to press. If closed, the **77 Garage** in Gisburn (3 miles) sells basics; open Mon–Sat 6:30am–8pm, Sun 7am–8pm; 01200 415953.

THERE AND AWAY
Train station: Gargrave (6 miles) – Leeds to Settle line. From Gargrave pick up the Pennine Motor Services bus no. 580 to Stirton and then the Lancashire United no. X80 to the site.

OUT AND ABOUT
Skipton Castle, Skipton (7 miles) – over 900 years old and still going strong, despite a history of sieges; adult £6, child (5–17) £3.50, U5 free, family £18.90; open March to September daily 10am–6pm (Sun 12–6pm), October to February daily 10am–4pm (Sun 12–4pm); 01756 792442; www.skiptoncastle.co.uk.
Narrowboat trip, Skipton (7 miles) – a 30-minute trip aboard 'Leo' on the Springs branch of the Leeds and Liverpool Canal adult £3, child £2; 01756 795478; www.penninecruisers.com.

open	All year
tiny campsites' rating	★
friendliness	☺☺☺
cost	BP ££, Couple ££, Family ££

As a campsite situated very much on the way to and from other places – it's just off the A59, eight miles from Clitheroe and seven miles from Skipton – it would be tempting to think of Rowan Bank as just a convenient stopover. That is, until you see the view. Off to the right stands the vast bulk of Pendle Hill, the first of a huge sweep of fells. The small town of Barnoldswick (if you ever need to pronounce it, go for 'Barlick') tucked under Weets Hill, completes a very agreeable picture.

The site itself is a simple one – an oblong field bordered by a low fence on a 40-acre sheep farm. There are some barns at the far end and a view practically everywhere else. Off site, Skipton offers a particularly good day out if you combine a visit to the castle with a boat ride on the canal; while walkers have a choice of tackling any of the hills they can see from their tents as well as the Easington Fell, to the north of Clitheroe.

The only drawback is that there's no loo here, so unless you bring your own you'll have to be prepared to sidle off discreetly into the wilds with a trowel, or use public facilities when you're out and about. Please also note that unless you fancy being sent to a farm several miles away at the top end of Horton in Craven, don't put Rowan Bank's postcode into your GPS. Stay on the A59 and, as long as you don't miss their signpost, you can't go wrong.

43 Crawshaw Farm

Back Lane
Newton-in-Bowland
Lancashire
BB7 3EE

📧 Martyn and Jayne Bristol
☎ 01200 446638
📧 jayne.bristol@virgin.net
OS Landranger: 103 (SD 693 514)

THE BASICS
Size: ½ acre.
Pitches: 9 (0 hard standing).
Terrain: Gently sloping.
Shelter: Low wall all round and trees
to the east.
View: Beautiful hills everywhere you look.
Waterside: No.
Electric hook-ups: No.
Noise/Light/Olfactory pollution: The
rooks sometimes like a good squawk.

THE FACILITIES
Loos: 1U. **Showers**: No.
Other facilities: CDP.
Stuff for children: No.
Recycling: Bottles, cans.

THE RULES
Dogs: On leads.
Fires: No open fires; BBQs off grass.
Other: No.

PUB LIFE
Parkers Arms (free house), Newton
(1¼ miles) – 'an inn for the way we live
and eat today' (make of that what you will);
open Mon–Fri 12–3pm & 6pm–'late',
w/es 12–'late'; food served Mon–Fri
12–3pm & 6–8:30pm, w/es 12–8:30pm;
01200 446236; www.parkersarms.co.uk.
Hark to Bounty (free house), Slaidburn
(3 miles by road, 1½ miles by footpath)
– lovely beer garden out back; open
7:30am–midnight 7D; food served
Mon–Sat 12–2pm & 6–8:30pm, Fri–Sat
till 9pm, Sun 12–8pm (breakfasts also
served daily from 7:30am – order the
night before); 01200 446246;
www.harktobounty.co.uk.

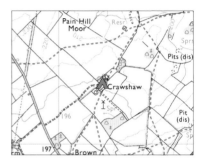

SHOP
Slaidburn Central PO (3 miles) – basics
and a selection of pies; open Mon–Fri
7:45am–5:30pm, Sat 8:30am–5pm, Sun
9am–2pm(ish); 01200 446268.

THERE AND AWAY
Train station: Clitheroe (7 miles) –
Manchester to Clitheroe line. From Clitheroe
take the Tyrer's Tours bus no. B10 to Newton,
a 20-minute walk from the farm.

OUT AND ABOUT
Bowland AONB – Crawshaw Farm is in the
heart of this Area of Outstanding Natural
Beauty, which covers 312 square miles of
rural Lancashire and north Yorkshire: the
vast gathering of fells, rivers, tiny villages
and wildlife is a paradise for walkers and
cyclists (see website for route suggestions);
01200 448000; www.forestofbowland.com.
Clitheroe Castle Museum (7 miles) –
recently refurbished 12th-century keep
with interactive museum; adult £3.50, U16
free; open daily in summer 11am–5pm;
01200 424568.

open	All year
tiny campsites' rating	★★
friendliness	☺☺
cost	BP £, Couple £, Family £

Crawshaw Farm is the sort of campsite Britons hold in their collective memory: a simple open field bounded by a drystone wall, with a loo in a lean-to by the farmhouse, and drinking water sourced from a tap coming out of a wall. A footpath goes right through the site, leading walkers off towards Slaidburn one way and Newton the other.

Kestrels command the skies above this 80-acre dairy farm, while tawny owls provide an aural backdrop at night. As for the view: bring along some extra superlatives because you'll be needing them. Even though Crawshaw Farm is 200 metres above sea level, whichever direction you look in you're greeted with stonking Lancastrian hills rising far above it.

Just a few miles away, or half an hour's walk via footpaths and a minor road, lies the small village of Slaidburn. A film-location spotter's dream, its stone houses and shuttered windows could easily stand in as a medieval French hamlet, so don't be too surprised if you bump into Audrey Tautou walking down the main street wearing a wimple.

Trivia-baggers will be excited to learn that the nearby village of Dunsop Bridge boasts a telephone box situated supposedly at the dead centre of Great Britain. Installed in 1992 as British Telecom's 100,000th payphone (ah, happy days), it was opened by Sir Ranulph Fiennes. Of course.

And please note that this is another campsite for which avid GPSers should take the postcode with a pinch of salt (it will take you off to Brunghill Farm, a mile up the road).

Ship Inn
Piel Island
Barrow-in-Furness
Cumbria
LA13 0QN

Steve and Sheila Chattaway
07516 453784
shipinn@pielisland.co.uk
www.pielisland.co.uk
Landranger: 96 (SD 232 637)

THE BASICS
Size: 1/10 acre.
Pitches: Variable (0 hard standing).
Terrain: Flat.
Shelter: To south.
View: Barrow, the Lake District, the Fylde coastline.
Waterside: A freshwater pool, plus the Irish Sea and Piel Channel.
Electric hook-ups: No.
Noise/Light/Olfactory pollution: No.

THE FACILITIES
Loos: 2M 3W.
Showers: 1M 1W (cold water only).
Other facilities: No.
Stuff for children: No.
Recycling: No.

THE RULES
Dogs: On leads.
Fires: No open fires; BBQs off ground.
Other: No.

PUB LIFE
The Ship Inn/Bunkhouse Bar (free house) opening hours 'flexible'; food served 8:30am–7pm 7D.

SHOP
Co-op, Roose Rd, Roose (4 miles from Roa Island) – small supermarket; open 7am–10pm 7D; 01229 822730.

THERE AND AWAY
Train station: Roose (4 miles from Roa Island) – Barrow-in-Furness to Lancaster line.
Ferry: Piel Island Ferry runs from Roa Island from 11am to 5pm, weather permitting; adult £4 return, U14 £2, U4

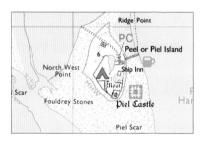

free; contact John Cleasby 07798 794550, John Warburton 07817 043385 or Steve Chattaway 07516 453784.

OUT AND ABOUT
Furness Abbey, Barrow-in-Furness (5¾ miles from Roa Island) – the majestic ruins of an abbey founded in 1123 by Stephen, Count of Blois (later to become King Stephen); adult £3.50, child £1.80; open daily July to August, April to June & September Thur–Mon 11am–5pm; October to March w/es only 11am–4pm; 01229 823420; www.english-heritage.org.uk.
Walney Island (1½ miles at low tide) – 'wet and windy Walney' has 2 large nature reserves and is home to the largest colony of lesser black-backed and herring gulls in Europe; www.walney-island.com.
The Dock Museum, Barrow (6 miles from Roa Island) – an innovative museum of local life inside a former dry dock; free; Easter to October Tue–Fri 10am–5pm, w/es 11am–5pm (last admission 4:15pm), November to Easter Wed–Fri 10:30am–4pm, w/es 11am–4:30pm (last admission 3:45pm); 01229 876400; www.dockmuseum.org.uk.

open	All year
tiny campsites' rating	★★★
friendliness	☺☺☺
cost	BP £, Couple £, Family £

There's something about Piel Island. Accessible only via a tiny ferry or a mile-and-a-half low-tide walk over the sands from Walney Island, its 52 acres comprise one medieval castle, one pub (whose landlord is recognised as the King of Piel), one brief terrace of Victorian houses, some grassland, a population of 'four, sometimes five' and a beach. Oh, and of course, in 1487 it was the scene of the last invasion of Great Britain.

While camping is allowed almost anywhere on the island, the 'official' campsite – ironically named 'The Crescent' (it's not a natural slice of suburb) – is in a slight dip and is further protected by shrubs, which help divert the Atlantic winds. The view is astonishing: a vista that stretches all the way from Lake District hills across Morecambe Bay, and along the Fylde Coast to Blackpool Tower.

The pub, the Ship Inn, has undergone a very thorough renovation and is due to reopen in 2010. In the meantime, drinks are served in the Bunkhouse Bar (expect to be joined by stray kayakers and yachters), while food comes from a trailer outside, also run by King Steve (a trained chef). His halloumi and sweet pepper wraps are delicious.

The castle is permanently open and free. It started life as a wool store, which, when constructed by monks in the 12th century, was the second largest building in Britain after the Tower of London.

Do consult Steve before attempting the crossing from Walney (possible for about four hours every day). Alternatively, local guide and nature expert John Murphy will take groups across (01229 473746).

Blawith
Ulverston
Cumbria
LA12 8EW

Mrs Linda Nicholson
01229 885277
info@birchbank.co.uk
www.birchbank.co.uk
Landranger: 96 (SD 261 875)

THE BASICS
Size: ⅗ acre.
Pitches: 20 (1 hard standing).
Terrain: Very gently sloping.
Shelter: Yes.
View: Great Burney and other hills to south; the Woodland Fells to the north.
Waterside: Smithy beck.
Electric hook-ups: 8.
Noise/Light/Olfactory pollution: No.

THE FACILITIES
Loos: 3U. **Showers**: 3U free (family room with loo & shower).
Other facilities: Washing-up area, washing machine, tumble-dryer, fridge/freezer, CDP.
Stuff for children: Building dams in the beck.
Recycling: Everything.

THE RULES
Dogs: On leads on fells (sheep).
Fires: No open fires – BBQs off ground (2 BBQs available).
Other: No.

PUB LIFE
The Greyhound Inn (free house), Grizebeck (3½ miles) – a pub run by the local community; open Mon–Thur 6–11pm, Fri 4–11pm, w/es 12–midnight; food served Mon–Thur 6–9pm, Fri–Sat 5–9:30pm, Sun 12–9pm; 01229 889224; www.thegreyhoundinn.org.

SHOP
Grizebeck Filling Station (3½ miles) – extremely basic supplies; Mon–Fri 8am–7pm, w/es 9am–6pm; 01229 889259. There is also

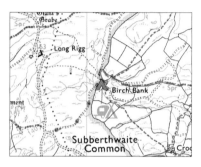

a small selection of shops in Greenodd and Broughton-in-Furness (both 5 miles).

THERE AND AWAY
Train station: Kirkby-in-Furness (5½ miles) – Barrow–in–Furness to Carlisle line. No onward bus service to the site.

OUT AND ABOUT
The Old Man of Coniston (Coniston start 8½ miles) – 803 metres of classic Lakeland fell. **Beacon Tarn** (1¾ miles) can be reached along footpaths, and the **Cumbria Way** (www.thecumbriaway.info) without touching an inch of road. **Coniston** – both the town (8½ miles) and the lake (3¾ miles at Lake Bank) are well worth a visit. John Ruskin's home, **Brantwood** (015394 41396; www.brantwood.org.uk) is best reached by taking the steam yacht 'Gondola' (01539 441288; NT site) from Coniston Quay; while the **Ruskin Museum** (015394 41164; www.ruskinmuseum.com) also covers speedster Donald Campbell and his ill-fated Bluebird; tinyurl.com/ycuqlgm.

open	mid May to October
tiny campsites' rating	★★
friendliness	☺☺☺
cost	BP ££, Couple ££, Family ££

Travel three or four miles inland from the Cumbrian coast, turn left off the main road and, coming over the top of a rise, there's suddenly nothing between you and the Lakeland Fells but a single long valley. Tucked under those same hills is Birchbank Farm, halfway along a picturesque road to pretty much nowhere (unless, I suppose, you live in the farm at the very end).

Set alongside the sheds on this 300-acre sheep and cattle farm, the campsite meanders gracefully down to a small stream called Smithy beck. There are free-range eggs for sale and, for a farm site, an unusually wide spread of facilities on offer. The washing machine, tumble-dryer and family loo/shower room make it especially attractive to people who are introducing their children to the delights of outdoor holidays.

The views of the surrounding hills are, of course, a constant enticement to get out and walk them. Perhaps the greatest draw comes from the Old Man of Coniston to the north, from whose summit Morecambe Bay, Blackpool Tower and even the Isle of Man can be glimpsed given a clear day. If your hiking horizons are a shade less ambitious, pick up one of the printed maps available on site. These mark out an easy circular walk to the remains of an ancient settlement nearby.

If you're up for a day by the coast, Kirkby-in-Furness and the delights of the Cumbria Coastal Way (tinyurl.com/yd4t4dw) are just five miles away.

Dalegarth Guesthouse
Hassness Estate
Buttermere
Cumbria
CA13 9XA

James and Kelly Gillings

017687 70233

dalegarthhouse@hotmail.co.uk

www.dalegarthguesthouseandcampsite.com

Landranger: 89 (NY 186 159)

THE BASICS
Size: ²/₅ acre.
Pitches: 35 (1 hard standing).
Terrain: Flat terraces.
Shelter: Yes.
View: No.
Waterside: 2 minutes' walk from Lake Buttermere.
Electric hook-ups: No.
Noise/Light/Olfactory pollution: No.

THE FACILITIES
Loos: 2M 3W. **Showers**: 1M 1W (50p for '6 min.').
Other facilities: Fridge/freezer, phone-charger socket, drying room, social room with pool table, darts etc.
Stuff for children: Rope swings, woods, fairy glades.
Recycling: Glass, tins, plastic.

THE RULES
Dogs: Under control (sheep about).
Fires: Open fires in fire baskets; slate available for BBQs (covered BBQ area at foot of site). **Other**: No.

PUB LIFE
A short walk along the lakeside brings you to Buttermere village and the **Bridge Hotel** – a rather swish affair; open Mon–Sat 9am–11pm, Sun till 10:30pm; food served 9am–9:30pm 7D; 017687 70252; www.bridge-hotel.com. Still rather nice, but not quite so swish or pricey, is the **Fish Hotel**; open Mon–Fri 10:30am–3pm & 6–11pm, Sat 10:30am–11pm, Sun till 10:30pm; food served 12–2pm & 6–9pm 7D; 017687 70253; www.fish-hotel.co.uk.

SHOP
Basic foodstuffs and camping equipment can be bought from a small onsite shop.

THERE AND AWAY
Train station: Maryport (18 miles) – Carlisle to Barrow-in-Furness line. No direct bus service to Dalegarth from Maryport, but bus nos. 77 & 77A (Honister Rambler) run from Keswick to Buttermere from April to October.

OUT AND ABOUT
Honister Slate Mine's *Via ferrata* (5¼ miles) – the 'iron way' is a route of supports in the rock face that can be climbed while safely attached to a cable: an exhilarating method once used by miners here; adult £25, child (10–15) £20, family £85; daily 9am & noon; 017687 77714; www. honister-slate-mine.co.uk/via_ferrata.asp. Fell walking – **Scafell Pike**, **Pillar** and **Haystacks** (Wainwright's favourite) are all within easy reach.

open	All year
tiny campsites' rating	★ ★
friendliness	☺☺☺
cost	BP ££, Couple £££, Family ££££

Buttermere was Alfred Wainwright's favourite lake, and anyone who has had even a minute's acquaintance with it will understand why. It's a comparatively small stretch of water by Lake District standards, but the reflection of the hills in its placid waters screams out to be photographed and stuck on the lid of a really expensive tin of shortbread biscuits.

There are very few properties on Buttermere's shores, making Dalegarth even more of a find. In woodland below the lakeside road, the sloping terrain has been transformed into three terraces of level camping ground, just two minutes' walk through trees to the shore, where one of the tastiest views imaginable awaits. Children are free to play in the grounds, where they will find rope swings and fairy glades in the woods.

The site (and attached B&B) was taken over in 2009 by James and Kelly, a young couple brimming over with enthusiasm and ideas. By the end of 2010 they hope to have converted one of the garages at the top of the site into a wet-weather hang-out for campers, with sofas, games and other little luxuries to make the wait for blue skies a cheerier affair. They can also supply filled baps for breakfast; sandwiches, flapjacks and hot drinks throughout the day; and packed lunches for whatever expedition you see fit to embark upon.

At night, the two pubs in the village of Buttermere lie a gorgeous 15-minute shoreline stroll away, past fluffy grey Herdwick sheep.

Holmpton
Withernsea
Yorkshire
HU19 2QR

Mike and Kath Cox

01964 630957

OS Landranger: 107 (TA 365 232)

THE BASICS
Size: ⅓ acre.
Pitches: Variable (room for 5 caravans and 5 tents; 1 hard standing).
Terrain: Flat.
Shelter: Yes.
View: The lights of Withernsea at night from farmyard.
Waterside: No.
Electric hook-ups: 6.
Noise/Light/Olfactory pollution: Light outside loo; the occasional neigh.

THE FACILITIES
Loos: 1U. **Showers**: 1U (50p – no time limit – pay on departure).
Other facilities: Washing-up sink; road bikes for hire (£1.50/hour).
Stuff for children: No.
Recycling: Everything.

THE RULES
Dogs: Under control at all times (horses around). **Fires**: No open fires; BBQs off ground. **Other**: No.

PUB LIFE
The George and Dragon, Holmpton (50 metres) – quiz night last Friday of the month; open Mon–Sat 12–2pm & 5pm–2am, Sun 12–2am; food served Mon–Sat 12–2pm & 5–8pm (Fri & Sat till 9pm), Sun 12–8pm; 01964 630478.

SHOP
Costcutter, Patrington (3 miles) – convenience store; open Mon–Sat 6:30am–10pm, Sun 7:30am–6pm; 01964 631315. There's a wide selection of shops along the coast at Withernsea (3½ miles).

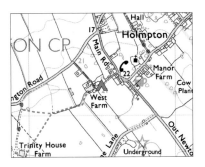

THERE AND AWAY
Train station: Hull (20 miles) – a terminus for various lines. From Hull take bus no. 76 (www.eyms.co.uk) to Withernsea, then hop on no. 71A (same company) to Holmpton.

OUT AND ABOUT
RAF Holmpton (300 metres) – a huge cold war underground nuclear bunker with café and cheery weapons of mass destruction gallery; adult £6, child £5, family (2+3) £18; daily tour (2:30pm) most days from March to October; 01964 630208; www.rafholmpton.com.
Spurn Head (10 miles) – an extraordinary 3½-mile spit of land shooting out into the Humber Peninsula, owned by Yorkshire Wildlife Trust – thousands of migrant birds and winter visitors land here, making it a magnet for birdwatchers; free (£3/car); always open; 01904 659570; www.ywt.org.uk/spurn_point.php.

open	All year
tiny campsites' rating	★
friendliness	☺☺
cost	BP ££, Couple ££, Family ££

This is unnervingly impermanent country. Villages around here have flourished, only to find themselves swallowed up by the sea. The fantastically named Ravenser Odd, for instance, which had its own MP and everything, now languishes under the waves a full mile-and-a-half offshore. There's something reassuringly solid, therefore, about Elmtree's Grade II-listed brick farmhouse. A small field around the back, its edges pleasingly tousled with hedge bindweed and house-trained nettles, has just enough shelter to make you feel snug without creating a sense of being hemmed in. The loo and shower, meanwhile, are part of the farm buildings, with easy access for campers.

The straggle of dwellings that makes up the unspoilt village of Holmpton is well worth a slow wander around. It is said to give a very good idea of what coastal settlements of times past would have looked like, and as such has been designated a Conservation Village. To see a number of really striking houses, take the more southerly of the two roads that lead straight out for half a mile to the sea. At the end, a footpath leads to cliffs above a long and (almost always) deserted sandy beach sweeping around to Withernsea, a small town three miles away along a cliff-top path.

The George and Dragon pub, being so close, serves as a useful annex to one's tent in bad weather and rustles up very economical bar meals as well as doing takeaways, particularly welcome after cycling the 46-mile National Byway loop (www.thenationalbyway.org) that passes through the village.

Bempton Lane
Flamborough
Bridlington
Yorkshire
YO15 1AT

David Southwell

01262 850536

woldfarmcamping@live.com

www.woldfarmcampsite.tk

OS Landranger: 101 (TA 217 722)

THE BASICS
Size: ²/₃ acre.
Pitches: Variable (0 hard standing).
Terrain: Pretty flat.
Shelter: On south and west.
View: Over fields to the sea.
Waterside: No, but just 400 metres from the sea.
Electric hook-ups: No.
Noise/Light/Olfactory pollution: A movement-sensitive light on the way to the loo; occasional braying.

THE FACILITIES
Loos: 1U. **Showers**: No.
Other facilities: CDP.
Stuff for children: Donkeys and sheep to stroke and feed.
Recycling: No.

THE RULES
Dogs: On leads and allowed at owners' discretion. **Fires**: No open fires; BBQs off grass (bricks available).
Other: No.

PUB LIFE
There are a dozen or so pubs in and around Flamborough, but one earning something of a reputation for its good food is the **Seabirds**, Tower Street (1½ miles); open 12–3pm & 5:45–10:30pm 7D (Sat till midnight); lunch served 12–2pm 7D, dinner Sun–Thur 5:45–8:30pm, Fri till 9pm, Sat till 9:30pm; 01262 850242.

SHOP
Co-op, Flamborough (1¼ miles) – small supermarket; open 8am–10pm 7D; 01262 850283.

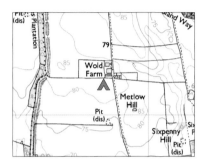

THERE AND AWAY
Train station: Bempton (3 miles) – Scarborough to Hull line. Bus no. 510 (www.eyms.co.uk) from Bridlington runs to Flamborough.

OUT AND ABOUT
Bempton Cliffs Cruise, North Pier, Bridlington (5 miles) – puffins from late May to mid July, skuas in September; adult £15, child £7.50, family £37.50; Sat only, advance booking advised; 01262 850959; www.rspb.org.uk/datewithnature.
Flamborough Head Lighthouse (3 miles) – built in 1806 and still very flashy today; adult £2.85, U16 £1.85, family £8; open April to September (not Tues), April 12–4:30pm, May to September 11–4:30pm; 01262 673769; www.trinityhouse.co.uk.
South Landing Heritage/Sculpture Trail, nr Flamborough (2 miles) – a mile-long walk through a nature reserve peppered with playful sculptures; free; always open; tinyurl.com/yc3qqry.

open	All year
tiny campsites' rating	★ ★
friendliness	☺☺☺
cost	BP ££, Couple ££, Family ££

Opened in 2008, this is a site for lovers of open fields and big skies. Three-quarters of a mile up a rough track, Wold farmhouse stands in wondrous isolation on the great chalk promontory that is Flamborough Head. The camping field enjoys uninterrupted views over the sheep-filled fields to both Flamborough lighthouses (new one on the left, old one on the right) with a sliver of sea to top it off. There's just one loo and no shower, so this is not a place

for luxury-seekers, but it's Eldorado for walkers and birdwatchers. Children too will enjoy the fact that they can stroke the farm's donkeys (including the elderly Bambi) and help feed the sheep.

Take the campsite's private footpath to the cliffs, just 400 metres away, and you can either birdwatch (puffins, gannets, skuas and countless others adorn the skies) or do the six-mile circular walk of the entire headland. Meanwhile, dipsomaniacs and those who just enjoy the odd tipple will be encouraged to learn that despite its apparently remote location, there are no fewer than 13 drinking establishments within a mile and a half of the site.

There are so many things to do in this corner of Yorkshire that the owners present campers with a welcome pack. It includes info on Sewerby Hall and Gardens (3 miles; 01262 673769) which in 2009 successfully defended its title as Britain's Best Picnic Spot. Take along a sandwich and a flask and find out what all the fuss is about.

Glaisdale
Whitby
Yorkshire
YO21 2PZ

Mr and Mrs Mortimer
01947 897516
Landranger: 94 (NZ 753 042)

THE BASICS
Size: 3 x ¼ acre.
Pitches: 25 (0 hard standing).
Terrain: Sloping parts and flat parts.
Shelter: Yes, lots.
View: Lovely Glaisdale.
Waterside: No.
Electric hook-ups: No.
Noise/Light/Olfactory pollution: No.

THE FACILITIES
Loos: 3U. **Showers**: 2U (30p – no time limit).
Other facilities: Recreation room with fridge/freezer, TV, washing-up sink.
Stuff for children: Slide and swing for U10s.
Recycling: Everything.

THE RULES
Dogs: On leads at all times.
Fires: BBQs off grass; open fires in designated areas (£1 charge; firewood available £1/bag).
Other: Quiet after 10:30pm.

PUB LIFE
Arncliffe Arms, Glaisdale (2 miles) – highly praised for its food; open Mon–Fri 12–2:30pm & 5–11pm, w/es 12–11pm; food served Mon–Sat 12–2pm & 6–8:45pm, Sun 12–2:30pm & 6–8pm; 01947 897555; www.arncliffearms.co.uk. The chef will give you a lift to and from the pub (he leaves the site at 6pm sharp), if you promise to order some of his food.

SHOP
Glaisdale PO (2 miles) – small convenience store; open Mon–Sat

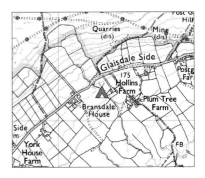

7am–12:30pm & 1:30–6pm, Sun 9am–noon; 01947 897244.

THERE AND AWAY
Train station: Glaisdale (3 miles) – Middlesbrough to Whitby line. Bus nos. 99 & 27 run from Whitby to Glaisdale; www.northyorkstravel.info/scarborough.php.

OUT AND ABOUT
Coast to Coast Walk – the 190-mile route from St Bees passes through Glaisdale (2 miles), around 15 miles from its finish at Robin Hood's Bay; tinyurl.com/yb76huo.
North Yorkshire Moors Railway, Grosmont (5½ miles) – an 18-mile line through the national park between Pickering and Whitby taking in *Heartbeat* country and *Harry Potter*'s Hogsmeade en route; day rover adult £20, child £12, U5 free, family £45; April to October several times a day 7D; November to March w/es only; 01751 472508 or 01751 473535 (talking timetable); www.nymr.co.uk.

open	Easter to October (can be later, weather dependent)
tiny campsites' rating	★★★
friendliness	☺
cost	BP £, Couple ££, Family ££

The most popular comment made by those arriving at Hollins Farm is reported to be: 'Ah, paradise'. It's easy to see why.

Three small plots are spread around the venerable farmhouse, so you can choose what sort of vibe you're in the mood for. The very chilled field at the top happily falls off a cliff halfway across, resulting in a very sheltered dingly dell below. A lower field is more attuned to families, with its own large shelter – handy for children to play under should it rain – and beneath which a fire may be lit at night. The smallest field, just below the farmhouse, enjoys perhaps the best of the Glaisdale views, although there's nothing to complain about in this regard wherever you pitch.

The farm is reached from a village (also called Glaisdale) by a minor road that climbs towards the head of the dale passing those Yorkshire staples, llamas and peacocks. It's one of those hidden valleys you would never know was there and is not on the way to anywhere, so it feels like your own private possession as you advance up it.

On site, there's something endearingly shambolic about the accommodation for the loos, showers and recreation room, for which all the available farm buildings appear to have been pressed into service. A swallow makes its nest in the shower room, unmatched chairs huddle around an old TV set (which bears the urgent injunction 'Do not bump!' on its side), while a small table-football game and other more or less random fixtures and fittings repose in far corners. Triffick.

50 **Park Farm**

Kildale
Whitby
Yorkshire
YO21 2RN

Mr and Mrs D Cook
01642 722847
parkfarm_2000@yahoo.co.uk
www.kildalebarn.co.uk
OS Landranger: 94 (NZ 602 084)

THE BASICS
Size: ⅛ acre.
Pitches: Max. 30 people (0 hard standing).
Terrain: Slopey.
Shelter: At foot of field.
View: West towards the far-off Yorkshire Dales.
Waterside: No.
Electric hook-ups: No.
Noise/Light/Olfactory pollution: Occasional bleating.

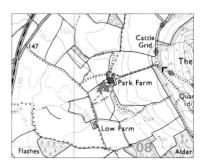

THE FACILITIES
Loos: 2U. **Showers**: 2U (£1 for 'about an hour').
Other facilities: Camping barn (sleeps 18; £7pp), tumble-dryer, picnic table.
Stuff for children: Can play in animal-free fields; bottle feeding of lambs on request.
Recycling: Everything.

THE RULES
Dogs: On leads.
Fires: No open fires; BBQs off grass.
Other: No.

PUB LIFE
The Dudley Arms (free house), Ingleby Greenhow (2½ miles by footpath and road) – bar meals, a bistro and a restaurant; open 12–2pm & 5–11pm 7D, w/es till midnight; food served Mon–Fri 12–2pm, 5–7pm (tea), 7–9pm (bistro & rest.), w/es till 9:30pm; 01642 722526; www.dudleyarms.com.

SHOP
There is a good selection of shops and services in Great Ayton (4 miles) including a bakery, a greengrocer's, an organic shop, a café and a **Co-op** – small supermarket;

open Mon–Sat 7am–10pm, Sun 8am–10pm; 01642 722219.

THERE AND AWAY
Train station: Kildale (1 mile) – Middlesbrough to Whitby (aka Esk Valley) line. Then a mile's walk onward to the site.

OUT AND ABOUT
Cleveland Way (¾ mile) – 109-mile trail from Helmsley across the North York Moors to Filey, on the coast; 01439 770657; www.nationaltrail.co.uk/ClevelandWay.
Gisborough Priory, Guisborough (9¼ miles) – a ruined Augustinian priory from the 14th century with a mysterious missing 'u'; adult £1.10, child 55p; open April to September Tue–Sun 9am–5pm (rest of year open Wed–Sun); 01287 633801; www.english-heritage.co.uk.
Roseberry Topping (3 miles) – a 360-degree view from the top of the hill taking in Teeside through to the Yorkshire Dales; 01642 328901; NT site.

open	All year
tiny campsites' rating	★★★
friendliness	☺☺☺
cost	BP £, Couple ££, Family ££££

Location location location? So very yesterday. It's all about view view view. And Park Farm in Kildale enjoys one of the most sublime you'll ever find on these shores. It's roughly 50 miles west to Tan Hill and the Yorkshire Dales, and on a clear day you can see absolutely everything in between: a joyous swoop of fields, trees and yet more hills.

The campsite itself is a tiny soft-cheese-triangle of sloping grassland bordered on two sides by a low dry-stone wall, with a hawthorn hedge on the third. A few cooking-apple trees give some additional shelter (and added pectin to your diet if you time your visit right) particularly at the snug foot of the field. The site forms a very small part of a 700-acre farm populated by sheep and interesting cattle (fans of Limousin, Shorthorn, Charolais and Belgian Blue bring your spotter books).

Captain Cook was born and raised in these parts (scenes for a film about his life were shot on the farm) and a walk up to the Captain Cook monument on Easby Moor (1¾ miles) is highly recommended, if only for the even more astonishing photo opportunities.

Meanwhile, loos and showers are housed in one of the many handsome farm buildings close by. Next door a fine-looking near windowless stone construction turns out to be a YHA camping barn (and a listed building to boot). Anywhere else and the heady mix of elevated sleeping quarters and flash fitted kitchen might tempt the camper inside. But then there's that view.

51

Highside Farm

Bowbank
Middleton-in-Teesdale
County Durham
DL12 0NT

Richard and Stephanie Proud
01833 640135
richard@highsidefarm.co.uk
www.highsidefarm.co.uk
OS Landranger: 92 (NY 946 237)

THE BASICS
Size: ¼ acre.
Pitches: Room for 8 people (0 hard standing).
Terrain: Mainly sloping.
Shelter: Some to the north.
View: North Pennines.
Waterside: No.
Electric hook-ups: 2.
Noise/Light/Olfactory pollution: No.

THE FACILITIES
Loos: 2U. **Showers**: 1U (free).
Other facilities: Washing-up room. Buy Highside Farm-reared meat for the BBQ.
Stuff for children: No.
Recycling: Yes.

THE RULES
Dogs: On leads.
Fires: No open fires; BBQs off ground (breeze-blocks available).
Other: No visitors; departures before noon; no arrivals before 1pm.

PUB LIFE
There are nearer pubs in Mickleton and Middleton-in-Teesdale, but it's worth your while going the extra mile or 2 to the **Three Tuns** (free house) at Eggleston (4½ miles); open Mon–Fri 11am–2:30pm & 6–midnight; w/es 11am–midnight; food served Mon–Sat 12–2pm & 6–9pm, Sun 12–9pm; 01833 650289; www.the3tuns.com.

SHOP
Stanhope and Weardale Co-op, Middleton-in-Teesdale (2 miles) – small supermarket; open Mon–Sat 8am–10pm,

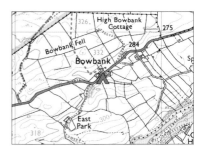

Sun 9am–8am; 01388 528219. Middleton also has a range of other small shops.

THERE AND AWAY
Train station: Kirkby Stephen (16 miles) – Settle to Carlisle line. Bus no. 572, run by Classic Coaches (01539 623254), goes to Middleton-in-Teesdale once every Wed.

OUT AND ABOUT
High Force Waterfall (9 miles by road or 5 miles by footpath); adult £1.50, U16 free; 01833 622209/640209. Or, for an even more spectacular waterfall, there's **Cauldron Snout**, 3 miles from the Cow Green reservoir (11 miles) up the Widdybank Fell nature trail (look out for blue gentian and the Teesdale violet in the spring); tinyurl.com/mjuan.
Raby Castle, Staindrop (13 miles) – a medieval castle and deer park as well as the setting for the river pageant scene in the film *Elizabeth*; ticket for castle, park and gardens: adult £9.50, child £4, family £25; open Easter & May to September (days vary according to month); 01833 660202; www.rabycastle.com.

open	May to September
tiny campsites' rating	★ ★
friendliness	☺☺☺
cost	BP ££, Couple £££, Family £££££

As evening wears on, all that can be heard from Highside Farm's campsite, on the lower reaches of Lune Moor, is the sporadic bleating of sheep far away across the valley. As the light fades into night, our woolly friends fall silent and the sense of tranquillity is complete.

There's nothing rushed about Highside Farm. Many of the farm buildings date back to the 16th century or earlier, and while the owners, Richard and Stephanie, haven't turned the clock back quite that far, they have become subsistence farmers on their 16-acre smallholding: growing vegetables and tending four breeds of sheep (including the rare Teeswater), some pigs and chickens. They also spin their own wool, balls of which are available for sale. Furthermore, if you order it the night before, they will serve you a breakfast packed with their own produce and locally sourced food.

An old stone shed has been transformed into two immaculate and homely loos, a shower and a washing-up room, while the campsite itself consists of one very small field with a static caravan just below it – perhaps the only visible concession to modernity – before the ground drops away rather dramatically, leaving nothing between you and the hills of the North Pennines to the south.

The Pennine Way (www.thepennineway.co.uk), perhaps understandably, rises near here by a rather less precipitous route and heads around the back of the farm, passing just half a mile away.

52

The Old Vicarage

Stotsfield Burn
Rookhope in Weardale
County Durham
DL13 2AE

Colin and Pauline Lomas
01388 517375
colin@finetime.wanadoo.co.uk
Landranger: 87 (NY 942 423)

THE BASICS
Size: ¹/₇ acre.
Pitches: Max. 20 people (0 hard standing).
Terrain: More or less flat.
Shelter: All sides.
View: No.
Waterside: No.
Electric hook-ups: No.
Noise/Light/Olfactory pollution: No.

THE FACILITIES
Loos: 1U. **Showers**: 1U (free).
Other facilities: Outdoor washing-up area.
Stuff for children: No (it's not really a site geared up for children).
Recycling: Everything.

THE RULES
Dogs: At owners' discretion.
Fires: No open fires; BBQs at owners' discretion. **Other**: No cars except support vehicles and small vintage VW campervans; advance bookings preferred.

PUB LIFE
The Rookhope Inn (free house; ¼ mile) – a walker-/cyclist-friendly watering hole; open 11am–midnight 7D; food served 12–3pm & 6–9pm 7D; 01388 517215; www.rookhope.com.

SHOP
The shop with no name, Rookhope (¼ mile) – very basic stock indeed; open Mon–Wed & Sat 9am–noon, Thur till 10am, Fri till noon & 3–5pm. Otherwise, try **Stanhope and Weardale Co-op**, Stanhope (5 miles) – small supermarket; open Mon–Sat 8am–10pm, Sun 9am–10pm; 01388 528219.

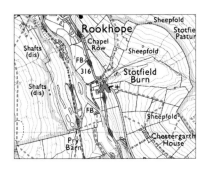

THERE AND AWAY
Train station: Hexham (18 miles) – Carlisle to Newcastle line. Bishop Auckland, on the main Tees Valley line, is 22 miles away. From Bishop Auckland, bus no. 101 travels daily to Stanhope, but it's a bit of a trek from there to the site.

OUT AND ABOUT
C2C – the 140-mile cycle route starts at Whitehaven, finishes at Newcastle or Sunderland, and passes through Rookhope-in-Weardale at around mile 95; 08451 130065 (Sustrans); www.c2c-guide.co.uk.
Killhope, the North of England Lead Mining Museum, nr Cowshill (10 miles) – a multi-award-winning 19th-century lead mine and museum; 3-day pass for museum and mine: adult £6.50, child £3.50, U4 free, family £17; open daily April to October 10am–5pm; 01388 537505; www.killhope.org.uk.

open	Easter to October
tiny campsites' rating	★ ★
friendliness	☺☺
cost	BP ££, Couple £££, Family £££££

Any cyclist or walker who has ever detected a smug look on the face of a passing car driver on a particularly draining hill, as the heavens have opened, finally gets to have the last laugh here, for this is a site dedicated to those getting around under their own steam. Thus, anyone thinking of rocking up here with a tent in the boot need not apply. The only circumstance in which a car will be allowed on to the hallowed driveway of the Old Vicarage is as a support vehicle for cyclists and walkers attempting a long-distance route (and then strictly one vehicle per team). As a concession to the petrol brigade, however (and because they look nice), small VW campervans are welcome.

The late-Victorian former vicarage is the possessor of a sort of wild lawn where feral plants outnumber blades of grass. This gives the camper the strange and far from unpleasant sensation of wild camping, while actually located in a garden. The feeling is intensified by the prowlings of Matilda, a hen whose determined and persistent enquiries as to the presence of food on your person are more akin to that of a grizzly bear, though, thankfully, she lacks the claws to back up her investigations with any degree of menace.

In the evening, candles on the tables give the site an undeniably romantic air, and if you happen to arrive too exhausted to put your tent up, you can always ask if there's a free bed in the vicarage, where they do B&B.

Slaley
Hexham
Northumberland
NE47 0AH

Elizabeth Courage
01434 673259
info@ryehillfarm.co.uk
www.ryehillfarm.co.uk
OS Landranger: 87 (NY 958 579)

THE BASICS
Size: ³/₈ acre.
Pitches: Variable (0 hard standing).
Terrain: Ironing board flat.
Shelter: On all sides.
View: Through the trees to hills and forests.
Waterside: No.
Electric hook-ups: 5.
Noise/Light/Olfactory pollution: No.

THE FACILITIES
Loos: 1U. **Showers**: 1U free.
Other facilities: CDP.
Stuff for children: No.
Recycling: Everything.

THE RULES
Dogs: On leads.
Fires: No open fires; BBQs off grass.
Other: No.

PUB LIFE
Travellers Rest (free house), Slaley (not in the village, but on the B6306 towards Hexham; ¾ mile) – beer garden; open 12–11pm 7D; food served Mon–Sat 12–3pm & 5–9pm, Sun 12–3pm; 01434 673231; www.travellersrestslaley.com.

SHOP
At the time of going to press, **Slaley's village shop** (1 mile) was due to close down. Assuming it has done, the nearest shops (and plenty of them) are in Hexham, 5 miles away.

THERE AND AWAY
Train station: Hexham (5 miles) – Carlisle to Newcastle line. Bus no. 870

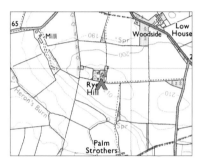

(see www.traveline.org.uk) goes from Hexham to Slaley a few times a day.

OUT AND ABOUT
Chesters Roman Fort, Hadrian's Wall (10 miles) – Britain's best preserved Roman cavalry fort; adult £4.50, child £2.30; open daily late March to September 10am–6pm; October to late March 10am–4pm; 01434 681379; www.english-heritage.org.uk.
Beamish Open Air Museum (21 miles) – a museum that takes the novel approach of telling the story of the people of north-east England by homing in on 2 years: 1825 and 1913; adult £16, child (5–16) £10, family £46, (in winter ticket prices are reduced to reflect the fact that fewer sections of the museum are open); open daily April to October 10am–5pm (last admission 3pm), November to March Tue/Thur/Sat/Sun 10am–4pm (last admission 3pm); 0191 370 4000; www.beamish.org.uk.

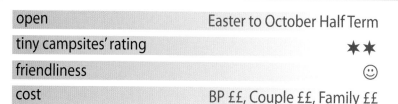

open	Easter to October Half Term
tiny campsites' rating	★★
friendliness	☺
cost	BP ££, Couple ££, Family ££

NORTHUMBERLAND

Northumberland, a strikingly beautiful county, can also be an inhospitable one at times. The people are lovely, of course, but the combination of the occasionally quite vigorous weather (as bemoaned by Roman soldiers on Hadrian's Wall in a million letters home to sunny Italy) and the austere landscape have lent the place a reputation as a wild, and sometimes desolate, region. This all makes Rye Hill Farm something of a surprise, because although it's set up high enough to command views around the countryside, its campsite is not some wind-blown wasteland, but a pleasant tree-lined area with grass so diligently tended as to tempt one to call it a lawn.

A long driveway from the road through the 30-acre farm ensures that the only noise disturbing campers is the hearty bleating of sheep and, since the owners don't like the site to get too crowded, it's unlikely you'll be unduly disturbed by fellow campers from your contemplation of Slaley Forest, a couple of miles off to the south. Furthermore, the free-range chickens that saunter around the site are not half as doggedly persistent as Matilda, the hen at the Old Vicarage (see p134).

Walkers have any number of footpaths and tracks to choose from in the locality, out to Blanchland Moor, the Derwent Reservoir and the woods of Dipton and Slaley. A little further afield, Hadrian's Wall beckons. Chesters Roman Fort is the closest highlight, with its wonderful Victorian museum bursting with Roman artefacts, though none of those mournful letters home.

Wales

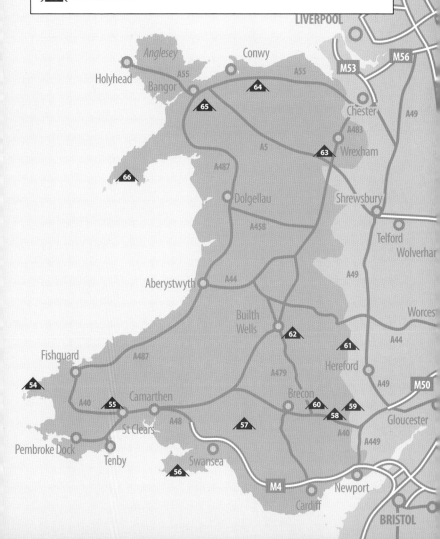

54	Porthllisky Farm
55	Glyn-Coch Craft Centre
56	Eastern Slade Farm
57	Lone Wolf
58	Middle Ninfa Farm
59	The Little Oasis
60	The Castle Inn
61	Radnors End
62	Trericket Mill
63	Ty Maen Farm
64	Gwersyll Maes-y-Bryn
65	Silver Birches
66	Treheli Farm

St David's
Pembrokeshire
SA62 6RR

Robin Elliott

01437 720377

porthlisky.cott@btconnect.com (yep, just one 'l')

OS Landranger: 157 (SM 737 241)

THE BASICS
Size: ⁶/₇ acre.
Pitches: Variable (0 hard standing).
Terrain: Flat.
Shelter: A low hedge on the western side.
View: Nearly 360 degrees.
Waterside: No.
Electric hook-ups: No.
Noise/Light/Olfactory pollution: No.

THE FACILITIES
Loos: No. **Showers**: No.
Other facilities: CDP.
Stuff for children: No.
Recycling: No.

THE RULES
Dogs: Under control.
Fires: At owner's discretion; BBQs
off ground.
Other: No.

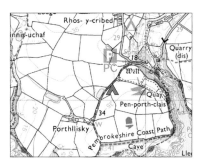

PUB LIFE
Farmers Arms (free house), St David's
(1 mile) – friendly pub with beer garden;
open 11am–midnight 7D; food served
12–2:30pm & 6–9pm; 01437 720328;
www.farmersstdavids.co.uk.

SHOP
St David's sports a range of mostly small
independent shops including **CK's**
(1½ miles), a large and rather funky
supermarket with a palindromic phone
number; open Mon–Sat 7am–10pm, Sun
10am–4pm; 01437 721127.

THERE AND AWAY
Train station: Haverfordwest (16 miles) –
Swansea to Milford Haven line. Bus no. 411

travels from the station to St David's, and
then it's a mile's walk to the site.

OUT AND ABOUT
St David's Cathedral (1 mile) – a place
of pilgrimage built on the site of a
6th-century monastery; free (guided
tour £4, booked in advance); open daily
9am–'after choral evensong' (which starts
at 6pm); 01437 720199 or 720204;
www.stdavidscathedral.org.uk.
Pembrokeshire Coast Path (100 metres)
– from St Dogmaels in the north to Amroth
in the south, the trail comprises 186 miles
of spectacular coastline, cliffs, secret
coves, sandy beaches, small villages and
the occasional castle, the vast majority
of which lie within the Pembrokeshire
National Park; 08453 457275;
www.nt.pcnpa.org.uk;.
St Non's Chapel (1¾ miles) – a holy well
and the ruins of the cliff-top chapel in
which St Non is said to have given birth
to David, who later became the patron
saint of Wales; tinyurl.com/ydpjtkl.

open	All year
tiny campsites' rating	★ ★
friendliness	☺
cost	BP ££, Couple ££, Family ££

Never let it be said that the St David's Peninsula is short of a campsite or two. Indeed, sometimes it feels as if it's just one large campsite. Such is the area's popularity, finding a field that hasn't become a temporary village can be difficult, particularly in the school holidays. Happily, Porthllisky Farm, being much smaller than its counterparts and a little off the beaten track, remains a little oasis of calm.

Indeed, despite being just a mile and a half from Britain's smallest city (pop. 1,800), just about the only sounds here come from passing gulls and the sighing sea. And then there's the view: a ring of mini mountains giving way to the stumpy tower of St David's cathedral.

The site is simplicity itself. Just under an acre of grass in a large open field on this potato-and-corn farm is mown to comfortable camping height. At one end there are some bins, while a water tap pokes out of a hedge. There are no loos, but 200 metres away at Porthclais Harbour (NT site) there are public conveniences that never seem to shut. There's also a very handy tiny café there that serves light refreshments outdoors, run by a very friendly chap called Steve (open daily May to September 10am–5pm 'and later if the weather's nice'; 07530 849078).

A special new path has been created through the farm to grant access to the nearby Pembrokeshire Coast Path, allowing campers to enjoy a spectacular circular one-day walk taking in the cliff-tops, a hill or two and St David's.

Ffynnongain Lane
Pwll Trap
St Clears
Carmarthenshire
SA33 4AR

Huw and Thelma Jones
01994 231867
glyncoch@btinternet.com
www.glyn-coch.com
Landranger: 158 (SN 259 175)

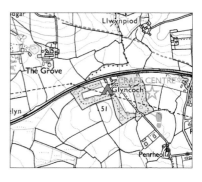

THE BASICS
Size: 1 acre.
Pitches: Variable (0 hard standing).
Terrain: Sloping.
Shelter: All around.
View: Llwyn Piod farm.
Waterside: No.
Electric hook-ups: 4.
Noise/Light/Olfactory pollution: No.

THE FACILITIES
Loos: 2U (in craft centre). **Showers**: 1U (free).
Other facilities: CDP, craft shop, woodland walk.
Stuff for children: Throw your own pot (£5); Wendy house in tea garden.
Recycling: Everything.

THE RULES
Dogs: On leads. **Fires**: No open fires; BBQs off grass. **Other**: No kite flying.

PUB LIFE
White Lion (free house) Pwll Trap (½ mile) – rustic country pub featured in the *Good Pub Guide*; open Mon–Sat 10am–11pm, Sun 12–10:30pm; food served Mon–Sat 10am–10pm, Sun 12:30–2pm & 4–9:30pm; 01994 230370; www.whitelion-pwlltrap.co.uk.

SHOP
Spar, St Clears (1½ miles) – goods store and off licence; open Mon–Sat 7am–11pm, Sun 8am–10:30pm; 01994 231322.

THERE AND AWAY
Train station: Whitland (4½ miles) – Swansea to Milford Haven/Pembroke Dock line. Buses travelling between Carmarthen and Haverfordwest stop less than a mile from the site.

OUT AND ABOUT
The Dylan Thomas Boathouse, Laugharne (6 miles) – the house where Thomas and his family once lived at the foot of cliffs on the Taf Estuary (there's a tea room too, though doubtless the poet would have preferred a pub); adult £3.75, child £1.75, U7 free, family £9; open Easter & May to October 10am–5:30pm (last entry 5pm), November to April 10:30am–3:30pm (last admission 3pm); 01994 427420; www.dylanthomasboathouse.com.
Pemberton's Chocolate Farm, Llanboidy (8 miles) – chocolate tours, chocolate cinema, chocolate museum, chocolate café and chocolate shop: not a place for the weak-willed; adult £4.50, child (3–13) £3.50, family £15; open Mon–Fri 10am–5pm (and w/es at Easter, summer and Christmas); 01994 448800; www.welshchocolatefarm.com.

open	April to end October
tiny campsites' rating	★
friendliness	☺☺☺
cost	BP ££, Couple ££, Family ££

It's a good job that the Glyn-Coch Craft Centre is well signposted, because it's a very long way from the usual tourist trail along which you'd normally encounter such establishments. Indeed, it's almost as though the centre wanted to avoid the passing trade, plonked as it is at the end of a very long, rutted driveway leading from a side road out of a tiny village.

As well as the craft centre (in which, should you feel the need, you can throw your own pot for a mere fiver) on your tent's doorstep, there's an oddly compelling collection of 20th-century technology (radios, computers, cameras, small farm machines etc.) and a tea room serving pasties, sandwiches and home-made bara brith (a kind of fruit cake). Outside, there's a woodland walk (adjudged the fourth best in Wales by people who judge this sort of thing) with two-and-a-half miles of pathway, while those with lepidopteran leanings will be excited to discover that the site is in the UK Top 20 in terms of moth diversity.

The craft centre stocks the work of more than 30, mostly Welsh, artisans producing everything from earthenware and art pottery to jewellery, buttons and pieces made from wool off the backs of rare-breed sheep, some of which live on this very site.

It's a pity about the electricity lines that fly near to one end of the campsite (and explain the 'no kites' rule). However, it is possible to ignore them as you look out over the 27-acre smallholding to a farm on a hillside opposite.

Oxwich
Gower
Swansea
SA3 1NA

Kate
01792 391374 & 07970 969814
tynrheol@hotmail.com
Landranger: 159 (SS 481 860)

Size: ¾ acre.
Pitches: 20 tents and 5 campervans (0 hard standing).
Terrain: Sloping.
Shelter: Low hedge all round but exposed to sea winds.
View: A fantastic seascape.
Waterside: No, but it's only a 10-minute walk to the sea.
Electric hook-ups: No.
Noise/Light/Olfactory pollution: No.

THE FACILITIES

Loos: 4U. **Showers**: No.
Other facilities: CDP.
Stuff for children: They can watch the cows being milked.
Recycling: Glass, tins.

THE RULES

Dogs: If well behaved.
Fires: Open fire in brazier; BBQs off grass.
Other: No.

PUB LIFE

Oxwich Bay Hotel (free house) Oxwich (1 mile) – the bar serves as the local pub and has a particularly pleasant and large beer garden (though they're a bit too posh to call it that); open Sun–Thur 11am–9:30pm, w/es till 10pm; food served throughout opening hours; 01792 390329; www.oxwichbayhotel.co.uk.

SHOP

General Stores (and tea shop), Oxwich (¾ mile) – very limited stock, but useful in an emergency; open February to October 8:30am–6pm 7D; 01792 391574. From

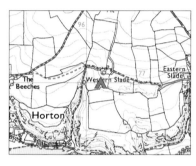

November to January, or for a wider range of comestibles, try the shop at **Knelston petrol station** (4½ miles); open 7am–9pm 7D; 01792 390903.

THERE AND AWAY

Train station: Gowerton (13 miles) – Swansea to Milford Haven/Pembroke Dock line. Bus nos. 117, 118 & X18 from Swansea stop ¼ mile from the site.

OUT AND ABOUT

Oxwich Castle, Oxwich (½ mile) – a stunning Tudor manor; adult £2.60, child £2.25, family £7.45; open daily April to September 10am–5pm; 01792 390359; www.cadw.wales.gov.uk.
Perriswood Archery and Falconry Centre, Penmaen (2½ miles) – birds of prey and outdoor archery (indoors if wet); 1-hour archery lesson £12, various packages available; open daily 10am–7pm; 01792 371661; www.perriswoodarchery.com.

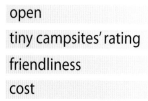
open	Easter to October
tiny campsites' rating	★ ★ ★
friendliness	☺ ☺ ☺
cost	BP ££, Couple ££, Family £££

There's been a campsite in this field on the Gower Peninsula for 60 years, and there are no prizes for guessing why. High above Port Eynon Bay (the climb up from Oxwich is not for the faint of leg), Eastern Slade Farm commands tremendous views across the Bristol Channel to Ilfracombe and Hartland Point in Devon. Even far-off Lundy can be seen on a clear day: look along Port Eynon Point to the Helwick marker, whose bell rings dolefully out in misty weather, and the island is beyond it on the horizon.

However, it's not just the views that make this a great campsite. For all their protestations that they are 'dairy farmers first and campsite owners second', the owners are extraordinarily sociable. They are often to be found around a fire of an evening offering an open invitation for campers to join them for a bottle of beer or a glass of wine. Their conviviality tends to rub off on all who visit, making this definitely not the sort of site where people use windbreaks to stake out their own personal fiefdom.

The rocky shoreline at Slade Bay is a 10-minute stroll away down grassy paths. The rockpooling opportunities are excellent and, most unusually for the Gower, the beach is gratifyingly underpopulated since it seems to be patronised only by those using the campsite.

The field is quite sloped, so be prepared to Velcro your sleeping mat to your groundsheet or put into action whatever other tactic you employ for such conditions; while four portaloos are the sum total of the facilities, but everyone seems to like it that way.

Lone Wolf

Lone Wolf Campsite
Glyn y Mul Farm
Aberdulais
Neath
SA10 8HF

Ian Wyndgarde
01639 643204
glynymulfarm@btconnect.com
(recommended means of booking)
www.lonewolfcampsite.co.uk
Landranger: 170 (SN 782 011)

THE BASICS
Size: 1 acre.
Pitches: 20 in woodland (0 hard standing).
Terrain: All sorts.
Shelter: In woods.
View: No.
Waterside: The River Dulais.
Electric hook-ups: No.
Noise/Light/Olfactory pollution: The rush and gush of the river.

THE FACILITIES
Loos: 1M 1W 3U. **Showers**: 2U (free).
Other facilities: Wash-room, kitchen with fridge, microwave, toaster, kettle, washing-up area, CDP.
Stuff for children: No.
Recycling: Everything.

THE RULES
Dogs: Under strict supervision (sheep on farm).
Fires: In woodland with moveable stone circles (firewood £5/sack).
Other: No music (apart from the odd acoustic guitar).

PUB LIFE
Dulais Rock Inn (Punch Taverns) Aberdulais (¾ mile) – also serves some takeaway meals; open Sun–Thur 12–11pm, Fri–Sat 12–midnight; food served 12–9pm 7D; 01639 644611.

SHOP
Ella's Store, Aberdulais (1 mile) – very small shop stocking basics; open Mon–Fri 8:15am–8pm, Sat 9am–1:30pm & 4–8pm, Sun 10am–1:30pm & 4–7pm.

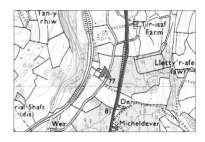

THERE AND AWAY
Train station: Neath (5 miles) – London to Swansea line. A taxi from the station to the site typically costs £8.50 – site owners provide tel no.

OUT AND ABOUT
Aberdulais Falls (1½ miles) – glorious waterfalls and some industrial history on the side, as well as the largest electricity-generating waterwheel in Europe; adult £3.63, child £1.81, family £9.09; open daily end March to October 10am–5pm (see website for other times of year); 01639 636674; NT site.
Afan Forest Park (12 miles) – 5 world-class mountain bike trails – from the 9-mile 'White's Level' to the dramatic 28–mile 'Skyline' – that draw riders from all over Europe; tinyurl.com/y8pze7n.

open	April to end September
tiny campsites' rating	★ ★ ★
friendliness	☺☺☺
cost	BP ££, Couple £££, Family ££££

NEATH

You can come to the Lone Wolf campsite and stay on one of its two small 'normal' fields if you like. However, if you do you'd definitely be missing out, because it's the woods that are special here. Crossing a single-track railway (it's for freight use only and the line can go weeks without seeing a train), you enter a much wilder world. You can pitch your tent wherever you like among the ancient wood of Welsh oaks and yellow archangels, by what was once a blue pennant stone quarry, but the most popular spots are those along the banks of the rushing River Dulais.

However, about one in five of the people who camp here don't even bring a tent, preferring to string up a basha or tarp across the trees and sleep beneath it, thus getting as close to nature as it is possible to be, short of simply lying down in a bush and having birds make a nest in your hair. Building open fires and engaging in activities that have a back-to-nature feel to them are actively encouraged.

Ian, the very friendly owner of the site, is a self-confessed 'recycling enthusiast', so many of the materials that have gone into the buildings that house the facilities first saw life elsewhere, which lends an esoteric pick 'n' mix feel to the place. Meanwhile, the loos, showers and kitchen are all just a short walk out of woods, making it a perfect place to hone your wild camping skills, while having a few home comforts close to hand.

Llanellen
nr Abergavenny
Monmouthshire
NP7 9LE

Richard and Rohan Lewis

01873 854662

richard@middleninfa.co.uk

www.middleninfa.co.uk

Landranger: 161 (SO 285 115)

THE BASICS
Size: 1/25 acre.
Pitches: 3 (0 hard standing). There are also 3 'remote' pitches further up the hill.
Terrain: Flat, but 1 pitch bumpy.
Shelter: Yes.
View: Vale of Usk and the Skirrid mountain.
Waterside: No.
Electric hook-ups: No.
Noise/Light/Olfactory pollution: No.

THE FACILITIES
Loos (compost): 1U. **Showers**: No.
Other facilities: Wood-fired sauna (small charge), fruit & veg for sale depending on season (sweetcorn, courgettes, tomatoes, spinach, chillies, rocket, hunter beans, damsons, grapes, apples etc.), maps of local footpaths to borrow.
Stuff for children: Tennis court, croquet lawn.
Recycling: Everything.

THE RULES
Dogs: At owners' discretion (sheep, ducks and horses around).
Fires: Open fires (wood £2 per bag); BBQs off grass.
Other: No.

PUB LIFE
Goose and Cuckoo (free house), Upper Llanover (3 miles) – cosy award-winning country pub ('Goose and Gander' map showing footpath route to pub available on site); open Tue–Thur 11:30am–3pm & 7–11pm, Fri–Sat 11:30am–11pm, Sun 12–10:30pm; food served 12–2:30pm & 7–8:30pm (credit cards not accepted); 01873 880277; www.gooseandcuckoo.com.

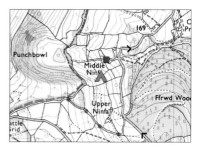

SHOP
Llanellen Stores, Llanellen (2¼ miles) – convenience store, newspapers, off licence; open Mon–Fri 8:30am–5:30pm, Sat till 1pm; 01873 852530. Abergavenny (2½ miles) is a market town with a wide range of shops.

THERE AND AWAY
Train station: Abergavenny (2¾ miles) – Newport to Hereford line. It costs around £5/6 for a taxi from the station to the site; tell the driver to go the Llanfoist way.

OUT AND ABOUT
Big Pit, Blaenavon (5½ miles) – join an underground tour of the mine and discover what it was like to be a coal miner; free; open daily 9:30am–5pm (tours from 10am–3:30pm); 01495 790311; www.museumwales.ac.uk/en/bigpit.
Llangorse Multi Activity Centre (16 miles) – go skytrekking, horse-riding, climbing; or get wet, muddy and impossibly disorientated tackling the dingle scramble; 01874 658272; www.activityuk.com.

open	All year
tiny campsites' rating	★ ★ ★
friendliness	☺ ☺ ☺
cost	BP £, Couple ££, Family £££

If ever a hill can be said to cascade down into a valley it's the Blorenge, halfway up which perches the smallholding of Middle Ninfa ('charcoal burner' in Welsh). From its three tiny and secluded wild pitches on the edge of the Brecon Beacons you can imagine yourself an eagle lording it over the Usk Valley.

A little closer to hand, though still far below, is the owners' cottage with its tennis-court-cum-croquet-lawn, next to which is a space for another tent or two. Even down here the view is an extraordinary one, off out into the blue and across to the Skirrid mountain.

Around the fire listen out for tawny owls in the woods, the occasional scream of a steam train's whistle and the crack of wood on wood if other guests are playing on the croquet lawn (or the crack of wood on scalp if things have become sufficiently heated). In the morning, expect a visit from a playful young cat and two exceedingly gentle horses – a chestnut and a grey – who are all happy to be made a fuss of and careful not to tread on anything they shouldn't.

A short trek upwards leads to a wonderful nature reserve and pond, while vertigo sufferers can check themselves into a luxurious bunkhouse by the cottage. Meanwhile, the site's eco credentials even run to a compost loo in a tiny shed in the garden.

And just in case all this were not heaven enough, you can book yourself a session in Middle Ninfa's very own wood-fired sauna. Just spare everyone the jokes about becoming a Ninfa-maniac.

Ty Newydd Farm
Pandy
Abergavenny
Monmouthshire
NP7 8DW

📧 Bill
📞 07851 644321
✉ thufir50@yahoo.com
🖥 www.littleoasispandy.co.uk
🅾🆂 Landranger: 161 (SO 335 220)

THE BASICS
Size: ¹⁄₁₀ acre.
Pitches: 7 (0 hard standing).
Terrain: Flat.
Shelter: From partial to complete depending on pitch.
View: The eastern edge of the Black Mountains.
Waterside: No.
Electric hook-ups: No.
Noise/Light/Olfactory pollution: Some traffic on road below.

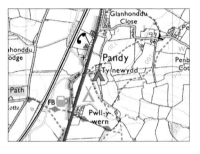

THE FACILITIES
Loos: 2U. **Showers**: 2U (free).
Other facilities: Washing-up area, picnic tables with shades, phone recharging, walking maps to borrow.
Stuff for children: No.
Recycling: Everything.

THE RULES
Dogs: Yes. **Fires**: Open fires allowed; BBQs off ground. **Other**: This is not really a campsite for children (though teenagers are welcome with their parents).

PUB LIFE
The Old Pandy Inn (free house), Pandy (¼ mile); open Mon–Thur 12–3pm & 6pm–'late', Fri–Sun 12–'late'; food served throughout opening hours; 01873 890208; www.theoldpandyinn.co.uk.

SHOP
Skirrid Mountain Garage, Llanvihangel Crucorney (1¼ miles) – small convenience store attached to a petrol station; open Mon–Fri 7am–6pm, w/es 7am–2pm; 01873 890275.

THERE AND AWAY
Train station: Abergavenny (5 miles) – Newport to Hereford line. It's best to take a taxi from the station. Buses run between Hay-on-Wye and the Old Pandy Inn on Sundays.

OUT AND ABOUT
Offa's Dyke Path, Pwll-y-wern (¼ mile) – the 177-mile route follows the ancient earthwork put up by King Offa in the 8th century and crosses the English–Welsh border countless times on its journey from the Irish Sea to the Bristol Channel; 01597 827580; www.nationaltrail.co.uk/OffasDyke.
The slightly less ambitious 100-mile **Beacons Way**, which scales the heights from Abergavenny to Llangadog, can be picked up a mile away at Llanvihangel Crucorney; www.breconbeaconsparksociety.org.
Abergavenny Museum (5½ miles) – set in the grounds of a Norman castle, the museum charts the disordered history of the local area; 01873 854282; www.abergavennymuseum.co.uk.

open	March to end October
tiny campsites' rating	★ ★ ★
friendliness	☺ ☺ ☺
cost	BP ££, Couple £££, Family £££££

'My biggest problem here', says Bill, the owner, 'is getting people to leave'. Campers, it seems, have a habit of booking in for a night and finding their tent is still in the same spot 10 days later.

The reasons for this are manifold. For a start, there's the fact that you get to choose the ambience that most suits your mood. The Little Oasis consists of seven tiny one-tent pitches, each quite separate and each with its own character. You can settle down next to the miniature meadow of wild cornflowers: corn chamomile, corn cockle and corn poppy; go for a sophisticated look on the terrace above the 17th-century cottage; opt for ultra-privacy on the 'honeymooners" pitch; or simply nab whichever pitch you consider has the best view of the nearby Skirrid mountain.

There's an eating-drinking-general-chilling lawn replete with picnic tables and parasols; an ambulance railway-van on tracks half-inched from one of the oldest railways in the world; a recently unearthed lime-kiln; and finally, that one thing that no self-respecting campsite should be without, a working model of a fulling mill ('pandy' in Welsh).

But perhaps the greatest attraction is Bill himself. A former actor and self-confessed 'gueller' (you'll have to ask), he seems to have packed several lives into his (not quite) 80 years and his fund of personal anecdotes – Corporal Patch, Richard Gere, Adam Faith, how Spot the DIY Dog rewired his house – is inexhaustible, making a chat with him a memorable event.

Pengenffordd
nr Talgarth
Powys
LD3 0EP

Jill Deakin
01874 711353
info@thecastleinn.co.uk
www.thecastleinn.co.uk
Landranger: 161 (SO 174 295)

THE BASICS
Size: ³/₅ acre.
Pitches: 30 (3 hard standing).
Terrain: Flat terraces.
Shelter: Yes, all round.
View: No.
Waterside: No.
Electric hook-ups: 1.
Noise/Light/Olfactory pollution: Some traffic noise from the A479, though this dies down at night.

THE FACILITIES
Loos: 2U **Showers**: 1U (free).
Other facilities: Washing-up area, picnic tables.
Stuff for children: No.
Recycling: No.

THE RULES
Dogs: Under control.
Fires: No open fires; BBQs off ground.
Other: No parking on grass.

PUB LIFE
The Castle Inn (free house) – log fire, real ales and general cosiness in what was once a farmhouse; open Wed–Fri 6–11:30pm or 'late', Sat 12–'late', Sun till 10:30pm; food served Wed–Fri 6–9pm, w/es 12–2pm & 6–9pm (Sun till 8pm).
The Mynydd Ddu Tea Rooms in Cwmdu (4 miles; 01874 731077) serve all-day breakfasts and home-cooked meals, and there are also some pubs in Talgarth (3 miles) when the Castle Inn is closed.

SHOP
Co-op, Talgarth (3 miles) – convenience store with a wide range of goods; open

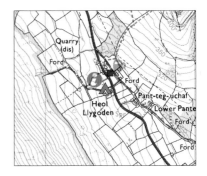

Mon–Sat 7am–10pm, Sun 8am–10pm; 01874 711311.

THERE AND AWAY
Train station: Abergavenny (15 miles) – Newport to Hereford line. Then hop in a taxi for the rest of the way.

OUT AND ABOUT
Welsh Crannog Centre, Llangorse Lake (4½ miles) – a recreation of a crannog: a house built on an artificial island in a lake or river, as used from prehistoric times all the way up to the Middle Ages; free; open more or less daily in summer 9am–5pm; 01874 658226; www.llangorselake.co.uk/crannog.html.
Crickhowell (8½ miles) – pleasingly old-fashioned small town in the Usk Valley with very ruined castle (free; always open), tea shops and spectacular bridge over the River Usk; 01873 811970; www.crickhowellinfo.org.uk.

open	All year
tiny campsites' rating	★ ★
friendliness	☺
cost	BP £, Couple ££, Family ££££

High on a pass on the western side of the Black Mountains – specifically between Mynydd Troed and Twyn Mawr – the Castle Inn and its banks of great willowherb are a welcome sight for walkers and cyclists at the end of a long day of heart-quickening climbs and perilous descents. The owners have also taken the trouble of terracing their campsite – top tier for vehicles, bottom two tiers for tents – so there should be no waking up at two o'clock in the morning three metres lower than when you fell asleep.

At the southern end there's a view through trees of Pen Allt-mawr and Pen Gloch-y-pibwr, two peaks that form part of a ridge that makes for an excellent day's circular walk. However, the majority of hikers who stay at this site are here for one thing: an assault on Waun Fach (811 metres), the Black Mountains' highest peak, for which the Castle Inn makes a perfect base camp. There are two routes up the mountain from here, so summit-baggers can walk up one and down the other. If that seems too energetic, the Iron Age hill-fort-cum-Norman-fortress of Castell Dinas is just behind the inn, and represents a rather softer challenge.

Mountain bikers, meanwhile, come here for the extremely taxing 25-mile Killer Loop (tinyurl.com/yeap329). It starts and ends at the pub, so anyone making it all the way round can either celebrate with a pint or slope off immediately afterwards to die peacefully in their tent.

Should the weather turn particularly waspish or some other such disaster occur, the pub also runs a clean modern bunkhouse and does B&B too.

61 Radnors End

Hay-on-Wye
Hereford
HR3 5RS

Mrs Zena Davies
01497 820780
radnorsend@hotmail.com
www.hay-on-wye.co.uk/radnorsend
Landranger: 161 (SO 224 431)

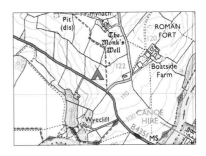

THE BASICS
Size: ¾ acre.
Pitches: 15 (0 hard standing).
Terrain: Flat.
Shelter: On all but the north side.
View: Terrific – over the valley to Hay.
Waterside: No.
Electric hook-ups: 13.
Noise/Light/Olfactory pollution: One lamp to light the way to loos.

THE FACILITIES
Loos: 1M 2W. **Showers**: 1M 1W (20p for '5 min.').
Other facilities: 2 washing-up areas, hot and cold drinks machines, fridge/freezer, 2 seating areas, tumble-dryer (10p for 15 min.), CDP.
Stuff for children: Small adventure playground.
Recycling: Everything.

THE RULES
Dogs: If well behaved and on leads.
Fires: No open fires; BBQs off ground (there are some square stones set in the grass).
Other: No.

PUB LIFE
The Old Black Lion (free house), Hay-on-Wye (¾ mile and a bit tucked away; ask directions when in town) – a 17th-century hotel and posh pub (booking essential); open 8:15am–'late' 7D; food served 8:15am –9pm 7D (Sat till 9:30pm); 01497 820841; www.oldblacklion.co.uk.
The Blue Boar (free house), Hay-on-Wye (¾ mile) – more of a pubby pub, is also recommended; 01497 820884.

SHOP
Hay (½ mile) boasts the holy triumvirate of a **Spar**, **Londis** and a **Co-op**, all of which keep long hours, as well as the delicious **Small Farms** shop (01497 820558) full of organic local produce.

THERE AND AWAY
Train station: Hereford (21 miles) – Shrewsbury to Newport line. Buses travel between Hereford, Hay and Brecon regularly.

OUT AND ABOUT
Hay-on-Wye (½ mile) – the town famously boasts more than 30 bookshops, the vast majority of them selling second-hand or antiquarian tomes, with over a million books between them. There's a helpful 'bookshop map' available at the campsite.
Paddles and Pedals, Hay (½ mile) – hire a kayak or Canadian canoe and head off down the River Wye (free pick-up from wherever you finish); Canadian canoe £30/£50 half/full day; kayak £15/£25; open Easter to October; 01497 820604; www.canoehire.co.uk.

open	early March to end October
tiny campsites' rating	★ ★
friendliness	☺☺
cost	BP £, Couple ££, Family ££££

What nearly everybody does as soon as they've settled in at Radnors End (not so much a campsite as a well-coiffed back garden) is lie back and soak in the views. Ask for a space on the south-eastern side, for there you can enjoy the panorama to the full: seldom since Simon Jones' performances for the 2005 Ashes-winning team has a combination of England and Wales worked so well (and, despite the postal address, the site is in Wales, not England). There's Herefordshire to the left, Powys to the right – in total a good 180 degrees of wonderful folding hills every shade of green, with the pretty (sorry, but that is the word for it) town of Hay in the foreground. Mighty Hay Bluff rises above the rooftops like a tricorne hat, with Twmpa (better known as Lord Hereford's Knob) to the south, with the Gospel Pass, the route to Llanthony Priory, in between.

Loos and showers are in a section of the owners' house, while there are two areas with chairs and tables – one inside a Portakabin (which conveniently also houses a fridge and drinks machines) and one just outside in the garden.

Despite the site's manicured and rather genteel appearance, the clientele tends to the more outdoorsy set, with Wye Valley walkers (www.wyevalleywalk. org), cyclists and canoeists eagerly setting up their little tents and chatting about their day spent in the hills/saddle/water before falling silent to gaze upon the lights of Hay coming on across the valley.

Erwood
Builth Wells
Powys
LD2 3TQ

Nicky and Alistair Legge

01982 560312

mail@trericket.co.uk

www.trericket.co.uk

Landranger: 161 (SO 112 413)

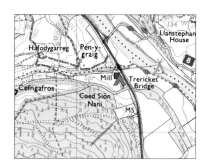

THE BASICS

Size: ¼ acre.
Pitches: 5 (0 hard standing).
Terrain: Flat.
Shelter: Yes, all round.
View: Up the brook and into the woods, depending on choice of site.
Waterside: The Sgithwen brook runs through the site.
Electric hook-ups: No.
Noise/Light/Olfactory pollution: Traffic on the A470, the gush and flurry of the small river.

THE FACILITIES

Loos: 3U. **Showers**: 2U.
Other facilities: Drying room, fridge, picnic tables; various foodstuffs available for sale.
Stuff for children: No.
Recycling: Everything.

THE RULES

Dogs: On leads (ducks and chickens).
Fires: In fire barrels (logs or charcoal £5); BBQs off ground. **Other**: Only campervans accepted are small vintage VW vans.

PUB LIFE

Wheelwright Arms (free house), Erwood (1¾ miles) – Victorian pub with restaurant and wood-burning fires; open 11–1am 7D; food served 12–8pm 7D; 01982 560740.

SHOP

Boughrood Stores (2 miles) – typical village store in a place apparently pronounced 'Bockrood'; open Mon–Fri 8am–1pm & 2–6pm, Sat 8am–1pm, Sun 8:30am–1pm; 01874 754300.

THERE AND AWAY

Train station: Builth Road (11 miles) – Llanelli to Shrewsbury (aka Heart of Wales) line. Bus no. X15 goes from Builth Wells to Brecon and will stop at Trericket Mill on request.

OUT AND ABOUT

Erwood Station Craft Centre and Gallery, Erwood (1¾ miles) – craft shop, gallery and tea shop with a resident wood-turner on a disused railway station; open daily 10am–5:30pm; 01982 560674; www.erwood-station.co.uk.
Wye Valley Walk (100 metres) – a 136-mile walk from Chepstow along the Anglo-Welsh frontier to the source of the Wye at Plynlimon; www.wyevalleywalk.org.
The campsite is very well placed for forays to the Victorian spa town of **Builth Wells** (8¼ miles), the riverside bookville that is **Hay-on-Wye** (9¾ miles), and the highly mooch-aroundable market town of **Brecon** (11 miles).

open	Easter to mid October
tiny campsites' rating	★ ★ ★
friendliness	☺☺
cost	BP ££, Couple £££, Family £££££

If a hen creeps up on your picnic table to check if any crumbs have fallen from your pizza, or you find yourself at your tent door watching a parade of ducks crossing a tiny wooden footbridge to graze at the water's edge, there's a good chance you're at Trericket Mill.

The mill in question, on the Sgithwen brook, ground its last corn in the 1930s but has been sympathetically transformed into a B&B with lots of the original machinery still in situ. The mill's back garden, a former cider orchard, is now home to a small bunkhouse and a lovely cosy campsite split into areas of varying sizes, so you can choose to be as private or as sociable during your trip as the mood takes you.

Cross the bridge and walk 100 metres or so upstream through the woods and you can avail yourself of a small plunge pool whose chilly waters are said to be invigorating by all who have survived them. Kayakers and canoeists, meanwhile, can head for the waters of the River Wye, into which the Sgithwen splashes a minute or two after passing the mill.

Avowed non-chefs can order not only a very reasonably priced vegetarian (or vegan) evening meal in the B&B, but breakfast the next morning as well. There's ice cream and pizzas on offer too, as well as pasta, sauces, baked beans and the like for those with a bent to rustle up something for themselves.

Pentre
Chirk
Denbighshire
LL14 5AW

Gail and Richard Lewis

01978 823184 & 07773 209403

Landranger: 117 (SJ 291 412)

THE BASICS
Size: ²/₃ acre
Pitches: Variable (6 hard standing).
Terrain: Flat.
Shelter: Mature wood on western side.
View: The A438 bridge, off to the east.
Waterside: No.
Electric hook-ups: 12
Noise/Light/Olfactory pollution: Some traffic noise and street lights.

THE FACILITIES
Loos (portaloo): 1U. **Showers**: No (but pending).
Other facilities: Free-range eggs for sale.
Stuff for children: No.
Recycling: Everything.

THE RULES
Dogs: Under control; ask for permission before taking dogs on to farmland.
Fires: No open fires; BBQs off the ground.
Other: No.

PUB LIFE
The Telford Inn (free house), Trevor (1¾ miles) – a picture-perfect pub at the northern end of the Pontcysyllte Aqueduct; open April to October 11am–11pm 7D, otherwise Mon–Fri 11am–3pm & 6pm–11pm, w/es 11am–11pm; food served 11am–9pm 7D April to October, & 11am–2:30pm & 6pm–9pm at other times; 01978 820469.

SHOP
Co-op, Chirk (2 miles) – mini supermarket; open Mon–Fri 5:30am–10pm, Sat 7am–10pm, Sun 8am–10pm; 01691 772979.

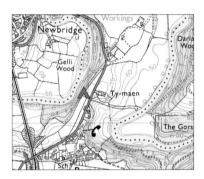

THERE AND AWAY
Train station: Ruabon (3 miles) – Shrewsbury to Chester line. Bus nos. 2 & 2A (www.arrivabus.co.uk) run frequently from Ruabon to Pentre.

OUT AND ABOUT
Pontcysyllte Aqueduct (1½ miles) – Thomas Telford and William Jessop's 1805 masterpiece on the Llangollen branch of the Shropshire Union Canal; free; always open; chirk.com/aqueduct.html.
Chirk Castle, Chirk (3 miles) – an extremely impressive 700-year-old fortress built by Roger Mortimer for Edward I; adult £8.28, child £4.14, family £20.70; open mid February to October Wed–Sun (plus Tues in July & August); variable opening times; 01691 777701; NT site.
AngloWelsh boats, Trevor (1¾ miles) – chug along the Llangollen Canal for a day; from £99 for up to 10 people; 01173 041122; www.anglowelsh.co.uk.

open	April to October
tiny campsites' rating	★
friendliness	☺☺☺
cost	BP ££, Couple ££, Family ££

Any initial disappointment at discovering that the slim strip of field given over to camping is severed from the farm itself by a road is tempered by the knowledge that here at Ty Maen you are not only in the hands of wonderfully friendly hosts, but you are also perfectly positioned for assaults on a veritable cornucopia of eclectic attractions.

The facilities here are undeniably basic: some recycling bins and a one-person portaloo (albeit a posh and immaculately clean one) are more or less it, though there are plans afoot to add a shower. Meanwhile, bat-lovers will be very happy to learn that some of the trees along the western edge of the field play host to boxes frequented by pipistrelles.

Across the road, Ty Maen ('Stone House') farm is populated by cows, sheep and pigs. There are no public footpaths through the farm but, on request, owners Richard and Gail will allow campers through the fields down to the River Dee, which all but encircles their land in a big lazy loop. They will also ferry car-less campers down to the pub and back of an evening if given a bit of advance warning.

Nearby there's the Offa's Dyke path, the Shropshire Union Canal (and its frankly unmissable aqueduct at Pontcysyllte), Chirk Castle, the Llangollen steam railway (www.llangollen-railway.co.uk) and the romantic ruins of Dinas Brân (www.castlewales.com/dinas.html). However, hang around at the site in the evening and you'll find the lights of the distant traffic on the A483 bridge make for a sight that is curiously compelling. Who says there is no mystery in modern life?

Carmel
Llanrwst
Conwy
LL26 0NT

Mr and Mrs G Griffiths

01492 640730

maesybryncampsite@hotmail.co.uk

www.maesybryncampsite.co.uk

Landranger: 116 (SH 836 637)

THE BASICS
Size: 1 acre.
Pitches: 30 (1 hard standing).
Terrain: Mainly flat.
Shelter: Most sides.
View: Denbigh Moors.
Waterside: At the foot of the site runs a stream called the Cyll.
Electric hook-ups: 10.
Noise/Light/Olfactory pollution: A light shines out from the loo.

THE FACILITIES
Loos: 3M (plus urinals) 3W. **Showers**: 2M 2W (free).
Other facilities: Washing machine (£1), tumble-dryer (£1), washing-up sinks, a few basic provisions for sale (long-life milk, cereal, soup, home-laid free-range eggs, toothpaste etc.), CDP.
Stuff for children: Playing in the stream, feeding the chickens, befriending the cats.
Recycling: Everything.

THE RULES
Dogs: On leads; owners must fill in a form accepting care and responsibility for their pets. **Fires**: No open fires; a supply of bricks for BBQs off grass.
Other: No cars between 11pm and 7am.

PUB LIFE
The Penybont (Scottish and Newcastle), Llanrwst (3¼ miles) – a 14th-century coaching inn serving cask ales next to a splendidly grim stone bridge rumoured to have been designed by Inigo Jones; open Mon–Sat 12–11pm, Sun till 10pm; food served Tue–Sat 12:30–8:30pm, Sun till 7:30pm; 01492 640202.

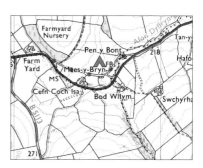

SHOP
Spar, Llanrwst (3¼ miles) – large convenience store; 6:30am–11pm 7D; 01492 640428. There's also a wide variety of shops in Llanrwst (though few open on Sundays, this being God-fearing country).

THERE AND AWAY
Train station: Llanrwst (3 miles) – Llandudno Junction to Blaenau Ffestiniog (aka Conwy Valley) line. Take a taxi from there on in.

OUT AND ABOUT
Llanrwst Almshouse Museum, Llanrwst (3 miles) – from 1610 to 1976 the building that generations of the deserving poor called home; adult £2, U12 free, family £5; open Tue–Fri 10:30am–3:30pm, w/es 12–3:30pm; 01492 642550; www.llanrwstalmshouses.org.uk.
Tree Top Adventure, Trefriw (6 miles) – high-level treetop thrills with zip lines and something called a POWERFAN™; adult £20, U16 £15; 01690 710914; www.ttadventure.co.uk.

open	Easter to October
tiny campsites' rating	★ ★
friendliness	☺☺☺
cost	BP ££, Couple £££, Family ££££

Welsh names, eh? They sound all mystical and dreamlike, but translate them into English and what happens? Ty Mawr becomes 'Big House', Hafod Uchaf is reduced to 'Upper Farm', while Gwersyll Maes-y-Bryn subsides into the disappointingly prosaic 'Field on the Hill Campsite'. Perhaps we'd all enjoy life more if we ditched English, a language no one wants to learn anyway, and conversed in the tongue of Dafydd ap Gwilym and Taliesin.

The former Dav yn Trap ('Horse and Cart') pub is now a smallholding with three acres' worth of sheep, chickens, geese, ducks and kittens. The very friendly Welsh-speaking owners really make you feel at home, while the site itself is separated into pitches on two levels, the lower one tending to be more sociable, while the upper terrace will appeal to slightly less touchy-feely types. There's also a miniature 'private' field to one side, right next to which sheep may safely graze, that can accommodate an extended family gathering.

Perched on a range of hills opposite Snowdonia, three miles up from the small town of Llanrwst, this location rewards campers with a fine view of Mynydd Hiraethog (the Denbigh Moors) to the north.

Llanrwst is worth a visit for its bridge, almshouse museum and plucky if slightly delusional sense of its own independence. The small town possesses a coat of arms and a flag, and glories in the motto *Cymru, Lloegr a Llanrwst* ('Wales, England and Llanrwst'). Local taxi firm Ken's Private Hire (01492 641010) will transport you from the campsite to the small Snowdonian republic for an extremely reasonable £2.

Cynefin
Betws Garmon
nr Caernarfon
Gwynedd
LL54 7YR

Ian and Marion Macleod
01286 650707
camping@silver-birches.org.uk
www.silver-birches.org.uk
Landranger: 115 (SH 544 567)

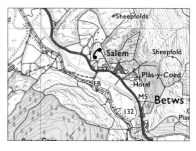

THE BASICS
Size: ¾ acre.
Pitches: 13 (2 hard standing).
Terrain: Mainly flat.
Shelter: Yes, though some wind from south.
View: Mynydd Mawr.
Waterside: A nameless stream near pitches 8 & 9.
Electric hook-ups: 3.
Noise/Light/Olfactory pollution: The fast flowing stream chits and chats its way over the stones.

THE FACILITIES
Loos: 3U. **Showers**: 2U (free).
Other facilities: 2 wash-rooms, 2 washing-up areas, washing machine, tumble-dryer, freezer, microwave, book swap, info leaflet area, picnic tables, hairdryer.
Stuff for children: No.
Recycling: Everything.

THE RULES
Dogs: On leads and by prior arrangement only. **Fires**: No open fires; BBQs off ground. **Other**: No children under 15. Cars off grass.

PUB LIFE
The closest pub is in Waunfawr (2 miles), but a much better option is the **Cwellyn Arms** (free house), Rhyd Ddu (3¼ miles) – a roadside inn with a log fire and real ale; open from 10am 7D, closing time depends on season (roughly between 9pm & midnight); food served 11am–9pm 7D; 01766 890321; www.snowdoninn.co.uk.

SHOP
Waunfawr Village Shop (2¼ miles) – village store with small off licence; Mon–Fri

7:30am–6:30pm, Sat 8am–6pm, Sun 9am–noon; 01286 650834. There's also the **Village Chippy**; open lunchtimes Thur–Sat and from 5:30pm Tue–Sat; 01286 650683.

THERE AND AWAY
Train station: Bangor (14 miles) – Chester to Holyhead (aka North Wales Coast) line. From Holyhead, bus no. S4 (www.padarnbus.co.uk) to Caernarfon stops at the site.

OUT AND ABOUT
Beddgelert (7 miles) – a charming village on the River Glaslyn that is well worth a snoop around; www.beddgelerttourism.com.
Welsh Highland Railway (nearest station Plas y Nant; ½ mile) – the world's most powerful 2-foot steam locomotives whizz passengers through some gorgeous Snowdonian scenery; return fare Caernarfon to Hafod y Llyn (just beyond Beddgelert): adult £25, 1 child free with each adult, additional children pay half-fare, U3 free; trains almost daily from April to October (see website); 01766 516000; www.welshhighlandrailway.net.

open	March to October
tiny campsites' rating	✦ ✦
friendliness	☺☺☺
cost	BP ££, Couple £££, Family ££££

Silver Birches is definitely a site for grown-ups. There's the book swap, the well-ordered pitches marked with bookees' names and the very civilised and wide-ranging facilities, but the clincher is the fact that children under 15 are barred from entry. Thus, it's no surprise that this site is very popular with teachers and others who, while they love children dearly, are very happy to be without their company every once in a while.

The lowering presence here is of the mountain opposite which, despite being a mere five miles from Snowdon, the Welsh still call Mynydd Mawr ('Big Mountain'). Behind, out of sight, is Moel Eilio, which is no shrinking violet either. The two serve as a palate-whetting hors d'oeuvre to Snowdon itself. The Snowdon Ranger path – one of the less-populated routes up Wales' highest mountain – is less than two miles from the campsite and, frankly, it would be rude not to take advantage of the fact, especially now that the £8.4-million summit café is at last open.

A regular bus service stops just outside the site linking it with Caernarfon, (whose castle is well worth a visit), the Snowdon Ranger path and Beddgelert.

Ian and Marion have thoughtfully produced a book of ideas for things to do in the local area that includes walks illustrated so well with their own photographs that they make getting lost the sole preserve of the preternaturally disorientated.

Treheli
Rhiw
Pwllheli
Gwynedd
LL53 8AA

Mr Williams
☎ 01758 780281
OS Landranger: 123 (SH 239 285)

THE BASICS
Size: ⁶/₇ acre.
Pitches: Variable (0 hard standing).
Terrain: Flat.
Shelter: Some on the north side, but very exposed to sea winds.
View: The whole of Porth Niegwl ('Hell's Mouth Bay').
Waterside: A 3-minute walk to the sea.
Electric hook-ups: No.
Noise/Light/Olfactory pollution: The long withdrawing roar of the waves below.

THE FACILITIES
Loos: 5U. **Showers**: 2U (20p for '5 min.').
Other facilities: No.
Stuff for children: Swings on trees.
Recycling: No.

THE RULES
Dogs: On leads.
Fires: No open fires; BBQs allowed.
Other: No.

The Sun Inn (Robinson's), Llanengan (5¾ miles) – friendly country pub with beer garden; open summer 11am–11pm 7D, winter Mon–Fri 12–3pm & 5–11pm, w/es 12–11pm; food served 12–2pm & 6–9pm 7D; 01758 712660; www.thesuninn-llanengan.co.uk.

SHOP
Ty Siop Llangian, Llangian (4¼ miles) – minimal stock; open Mon–Tue & Thur–Fri 7:30am–noon & 1–5pm; Wed & w/es 7:30am–noon; 01758 712095. There is also a small store at Aberdaron (5 miles) and a variety of shops at the attractive resort town of Abersoch (6 miles).

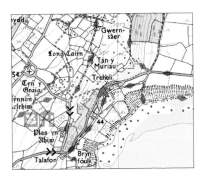

THERE AND AWAY
Train station: Pwllheli (10 miles) – Pwllheli to Shrewsbury line. Bus no. 17B from Pwllheli stops down the lane from the site.

OUT AND ABOUT
Plas yn Rhiw (¼ mile) – a splendid little manor house with a fine ornamental garden; adult £4, child £2, family £10; open April to September Thur–Sun 12–5pm (plus some Mon & Wed), October to November Thur–Sun 12–4pm; 01758 780219; NT site.
The beach at **Porth Ysgo** (3½ miles) is renowned among the climbing set for its curious but highly scalable gabbro boulders; tinyurl.com/y8plfj7.

open	Easter to October
tiny campsites' rating	✸ ✸
friendliness	☺
cost	BP £££, Couple £££, Family £££

Arguably the ultimate expression of the tiny campsite: not only is Treheli already admirably compact, but it's actually getting smaller every year. Perched above Hell's Mouth Bay, the cliffs beneath it are so friable that over the years its three tiers have been reduced to one, and the time is coming when that too will have crumbled away and the campsite will disappear.

So, there's no time to waste if you wish to sample the uninterrupted sea views; the precipitous three-minute walk down to the sandy beach; the sheep being driven right through the site of an evening; the chance visits from pheasants; the determinedly rustic facilities (mystifyingly there's no loo roll provided, so remember to take your own) and the informal cliff-top camping experience. The total lack of signage to – and even at – the farm means that you'll be advised to take a map along too.

The locals acknowledge that there is something of a dearth of good pubs in the vicinity (and a complete absence of them close by) until you reach the Sun Inn at Llanengan. It's nearly six miles by road, but if you walk there via the beach (making sure to avoid high tide) it cuts it down to about four, and makes for a bracing pre-prandial stroll.

Sadly, the rigidly enforced flat fee per group, regardless of size, puts Treheli in the running for the title of 'Britain's Most Expensive Site for the Solo Camper'. On the upside, if you were to pack a couple of enormo-tents and take along everyone you know, you could enjoy the cheapest holiday imaginable.

Scotland

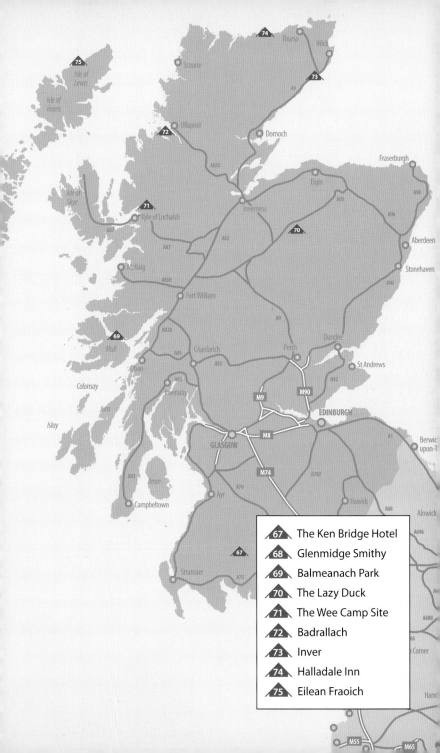

Scourie

Thurso

Wick

Isle of
Lewis

Isle of
Harris

Ullapool

Dornoch

Fraserburgh

Isle of
Skye

Kyle of Lochalsh

Elgin

Inverness

Aberdeen

Mallaig

Fort William

Stonehaven

Mull

Crianlarich

Dundee

Perth

St Andrews

Colonsay

Oban

Inveraray

Jura

Islay

EDINBURGH

Berwick
upon-T

GLASGOW

Arran

Ayr

Hawick

Alnwick

Campbeltown

Stranraer

67	The Ken Bridge Hotel
68	Glenmidge Smithy
69	Balmeanach Park
70	The Lazy Duck
71	The Wee Camp Site
72	Badrallach
73	Inver
74	Halladale Inn
75	Eilean Fraoich

67 The Ken Bridge Hotel

New Galloway
Dumfries and Galloway
DG7 3PR

Dave and Sue Paterson
01644 420211
mail@kenbridgehotel.co.uk
www. kenbridgehotel.co.uk
Landranger: 83 (NX 641 783)

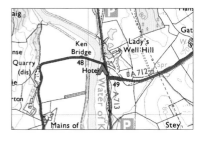

THE BASICS
Size: ½ acre.
Pitches: Variable; 'we don't like to overcrowd it' (0 hard standing).
Terrain: Mainly flat.
Shelter: Yes.
View: Ken Bridge.
Waterside: Yes, the Water of Ken.
Electric hook-ups: 5.
Noise/Light/Olfactory pollution: No.

THE FACILITIES
Loos: 2U. **Showers**: 1U (free).
Other facilities: CDP.
Stuff for children: No.
Recycling: Bottles, cans, paper.

THE RULES
Dogs: No dogs.
Fires: No open fires; BBQs well off ground.
Other: No.

PUB LIFE
The Ken Bridge Hotel (free house) – during summer it's open throughout the day for cream teas and snacks including soup, chips and sandwiches; open 11am–midnight 7D; meals served 12–2pm & 5:30–8:30pm 7D.

SHOP
JR Hopkins, New Galloway (1 mile) – basics plus some fruit & veg; open Mon–Fri 7:30am–5:30pm, Sat 8am–5pm, Sun 8:30am–1pm; 01644 420229. There is also a small shop up the hill in Balmaclellan (1 mile) – closed Sun – and a clog and shoe workshop.

THERE AND AWAY
Train station: Dumfries (24 miles) – Glasgow Central to Carlisle line. A regular bus service from Dumfries stops right outside the hotel.

OUT AND ABOUT
Southern Upland Way – Scotland's 212-mile coast-to-coast trail passes close by at the wonderfully named St John's Town of Dalry (2½ miles); www.southernuplandway.gov.uk.
Loch Ken (4 miles) – sailing, windsurfing, kayaking, canoeing, climbing, archery and (of course) an outdoor laser quest; 01644 420626; www.lochken.co.uk.
Seven Stanes (various distances) – 5 of the 7 Stanes, which offer some of the best mountain bike trails in Britain, are within striking distance of the site; 01387 272440; www.7stanes.gov.uk.

open	All year (depending on river)
tiny campsites' rating	✳ ✳ ✳
friendliness	☺☺☺
cost	BP ££, Couple ££, Family ££

Deep in the heart of Dumfries and Galloway runs the wondrously named Water of Ken. At the elegant Ken Bridge, just 10 miles from the river's source, it already demands five full spans to cross it, having by then incorporated the rivers Dee, Doon and Deugh. Beside the Ken Bridge stands an 18th-century coaching inn whose lovely diminutive beer garden extends, apparently unwittingly, into a small riverside field. This, it turns out, is the campsite, and the combination of river, welcoming pub and surrounding hills makes it a little cracker.

There are otters in the river and if you wish to compete with them for food, including the invasive crayfish, the fishing is free for campers. Bird-lovers, meanwhile, can look out for kingfishers and ospreys on the Ken or follow the nearby Galloway Kite Trail, a circular route that takes in the best places to see these magnificent birds of prey, which have recently been successfully reintroduced to the area.

New Galloway (the smallest royal borough in Scotland, fact fans) is only a mile away and, though just a wee village, it boasts a highly regarded arts performance space called CatStrand (01644 420374) whose varied programme is always worth checking.

Further afield, Wigtown (25 miles) is Scotland's 'National Book Town' (look out, Hay). There's an annual 10-day literary festival at the end of September (www.wigtownbookfestival.com) and, as you might expect, the place is bursting at the seams with bookshops, both second-hand and new.

68 Glenmidge Smithy

Auldgirth
Dumfries and Galloway
DG2 0SW

James (aka Hamish) and Margaret Steele
01387 740328
Landranger: 78 (NX 891 870)

THE BASICS
Size: ½ acre.
Pitches: Variable (3 hard standing).
Terrain: Flat.
Shelter: Yes.
View: Hills.
Waterside: A nameless burn runs by.
Electric hook-ups: 16.
Noise/Light/Olfactory pollution: No.

THE FACILITIES
Loos: 1U. **Showers**: 1U (free).
Other facilities: Washing-up area, electric hob, microwave, kettle, toaster, table and chairs, fridge, tourist information, washing machine, CDP, owners' honey for sale.
Stuff for children: No.
Recycling: Everything.

THE RULES
Dogs: On leads (there's a doggy run around the corner).
Fires: No open fires; BBQs off ground (bricks may be borrowed).
Other: Adults only (16+) on site.

PUB LIFE
Auldgirth Inn (free house; 2 miles) – a friendly pub on the edge of the village; open Mon–Tue 5pm–midnight, Wed–Fri 12–2:30pm & 5pm–midnight, w/es 12–midnight; food served Mon–Tue 5:30–8:30pm, Wed–Fri 12–2pm & 5:30–8:30pm, Sat 12–8:30pm, Sun till 8pm; 01387 740250; www.auldgirthinn.co.uk.

SHOP
Auldgirth Stores (1¾ miles) – basics plus some fruit & veg with tea room/bistro attached; open Mon–Sat 7:30am–6pm, Sun 9am–4pm (till noon in winter); tea room/bistro open Mon–Thur 7:30am–8pm, Fri till 9pm, Sat 9am–9pm, Sun 11am–8pm; 01387 740235.

THERE AND AWAY
Train station: Dumfries (8 miles) – Glasgow to Carlisle line. Bus no. 236 from Dumfries stops at Auldgirth.

OUT AND ABOUT
Drumlanrig Castle (9 miles) – a late-17th-century castle in the Renaissance style, country estate, cycle museum, gardens and home to the Buccleuch art collection; adult £8, child (3–16) £4.50, family £23; castle open daily April to September 11am–4pm; 01848 331555; www.drumlanrig.com.
Seven Stanes (various distances; see the Ken Bridge Hotel entry, p168). Hire bikes from Rik's Bike Shed and Cycle Museum at Drumlanrig Castle; 01848 330080.

open	March to November
tiny campsites' rating	★ ★
friendliness	☺☺
cost	BP £, Couple ££, Family £££

The hamlet of Glenmidge, 11 miles north of Dumfries, is hidden in a complex network of narrow roads spread around farms that sprawl over low tumbling hills. The former blacksmith's house in the settlement now hosts a small, well-sheltered campsite with a view over the hedge to some of those hills and access to more prime cycling country than is either good or proper.

A building that might be either a small barn or a large shed has been kitted out with every mod con, including a dining area – a boon for those one or two days a year when Scotland experiences rain. The barn/shed also contains handy maps of the local area for those wanting to walk or cycle. At night, though, you can just lie back and watch the stars come out to shine; laminated charts are available to help you sort your Ursa Major from your Andromeda.

Happily, Glenmidge does not owe its name to the small biting insect for which Scotland is rightly famous, but is derived from the Gaelic for 'small glen'. Like the rest of Scotland (and, lest we forget, parts of the far north of England), the site is susceptible to the odd midge in summer, but only on days when there is no wind (see Top Tips, p11, for midge-repelling strategies).

This quiet site is for adults only, though as children are assumed to have morphed into adults by the time they are 16, this means that parents can take along any older teenagers who still deign to holiday with them.

Fishnish
Aros
Isle of Mull
PA65 6BA

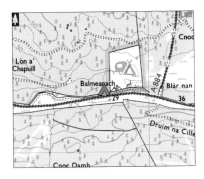

Cynthia and Alex MacFadyen

01680 300342

www.holidaymull.co.uk/minisites/balmeanach

Landranger: 49 (NM 657 414)

THE BASICS
Size: 1 acre.
Pitches: 15 (6 hard standing).
Terrain: Some flat, some slightly sloping pitches.
Shelter: Yes.
View: Fishnish Forest.
Waterside: A tiny stream runs through the site.
Electric hook-ups: 4.
Noise/Light/Olfactory pollution: Occasional traffic on road, but this is barely audible from the more distant pitches.

THE FACILITIES
Loos: 2U. **Showers**: 1U (free).
Other facilities: Washing-up area, clothes washing area, tumble-dryer.
Stuff for children: No.
Recycling: Everything.

THE RULES
Dogs: On leads; max. 2 per pitch.
Fires: No open fires; BBQs off grass.
Other: No.

PUB LIFE
Craignure Inn (free house; 5¾ miles) – 18th-century drovers' inn with lots of locally produced food on the menu and frequent live music; open 11–1am 7D; food served 8:30–11am & 11:30am–10:30pm 7D (shorter hours in winter); 01680 812305; www.craignure-inn.co.uk.
Or for something a little more modern, you could try **Macgregor's Roadhouse** (free house), Craignure (5¾ miles) – open 9am–'late'; breakfast served 9–11:30am, lunch 11:30am–2:30pm, dinner 5–9pm 7D (shorter hours in winter); 01680 812471.

SHOP
Craignure Stores (Spar) (5¾ miles) – convenience store; open Mon–Sat 8am–6pm, Sun 10am–6pm; 01680 812301.

THERE AND AWAY
Ferry terminal: Fishnish (1 mile) for the short hop over to Lochaline on the mainland; or Craignure (5¾ miles) for the longer trip to Oban, where there is a train station; Caledonian MacBrayne ferries 08000 665000; www.calmac.co.uk. The bus from Craignure to Tobermory stops at the site.

OUT AND ABOUT
Tobermory (18 miles) – the fishing community whose gaily painted houses have graced coffee tables, calendars and, in the guise of *Balamory*, children's television schedules; www.tobermory.co.uk.
Iona (43 miles) – a bit of a trek along Mull's single-track roads, but well worth it to visit this tiny island and its abbey founded by St Columba; www.isle-of-iona.com.

open	mid April to mid October
tiny campsites' rating	★ ★
friendliness	☺☺
cost	BP ££, Couple £££, Family ££££

There's a good deal to recommend Mull. Not only is it full of the open spaces you expect on an Inner Hebridean island, but it also runs to some fantastic little communities, as well as being the place to spot all manner of Scotland's choicest wildlife including sea eagles, golden eagles, otters and seals.

Set within Fishnish Forest, Balmeanach Park extends over seven acres, including a wildflower woodland garden. The campsite itself is divided in two. The first section, just past the loos and shower, has been very carefully laid out and is mainly for campervans and caravans. However, pass through this and head across a wee footbridge, and you'll find a host of little individual camping pitches to choose from in a slightly wilder area offering views of Fishnish Forest to the north.

There are signposted forest walks close by, while a 20-minute stroll will take you to the shoreline of the Sound of Mull and a view across to the mainland. Should you fancy a bit of culture, there's a thriving and highly regarded theatre (www.mulltheatre.com) at Druimfin, near Tobermory.

The campsite is extremely handy for the Fishnish ferry terminal (in reality, not much more than a jetty and a shelter) but if, like most visitors, you sail from Oban and land at Craignure, a bus service (tinyurl.com/yzchlsn) will whisk you to the site in 10 minutes before rattling along to the bright lights of Tobermory, with its distillery and little folk museum (www.mullmuseum.org.uk).

Nethy Bridge
Inverness-shire
PH25 3ED

David and Valery Dean

lazyduckhostel@googlemail.com

www.lazyduck.co.uk

Landranger: 36 (NJ 016 204)

THE BASICS
Size: ⅕ acre.
Pitches: 4 (0 hard standing).
Terrain: Slightly undulating.
Shelter: Yes.
View: Field with Soay sheep, geese and hens.
Waterside: Burn and ponds.
Electric hook-ups: No.
Noise/Light/Olfactory pollution: No.

THE FACILITIES
Loos: 1U. **Showers** (outdoor 'bush' shower): 1U (free).
Other facilities: Washing-up area, campers' shelter, picnic table, chimenea, eggs and veg (in season) for sale, a gorgeous Swiss-style hostel.
Stuff for children: 2 swings, 2 hammocks, red squirrel feeding station, a bit of duck feeding on request. **Recycling**: Everything.

THE RULES
Dogs: No dogs. **Fires**: In chimenea only; BBQs off ground (stands available).
Other: Don't disturb the lazy ducks.

PUB LIFE
The Old Bridge Inn, Aviemore (11½ miles) – cheery open fire and outdoorsy punters aplenty; open Mon–Thur 12–11pm, Fri & Sat till midnight, Sun 12:30–11pm; food served 12–2pm & 6–9pm 7D (Fri & Sat till 9:30pm); 01479 811137; www.oldbridgeinn.co.uk.

SHOP
Nethy Bridge Village Store (Spar; 1 mile) – comprehensively stocked convenience store and PO; Mon–Sat 8am–6pm, Sun 9am–6pm; 01479 821217.

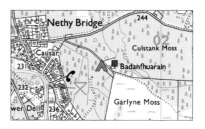

THERE AND AWAY
Train station: Carrbridge or Aviemore (10/12 miles) – Perth to Inverness line. Highland Country Buses (01479 811211) run to Nethy Bridge from Aviemore.

OUT AND ABOUT
Speyside Way – the 65-mile path from Buckie, on the Moray Firth, to Aviemore passes through Nethy Bridge (1 mile); 01340 881266; www.speysideway.org. The local area is also criss-crossed with footpaths for shorter wanders; www.exploreabernethy.co.uk.
National Cycle Route No. 7 (Inverness–Sunderland) passes through Boat of Garten (5½ miles) and is joined by numerous other local on-road and off-road cycle trails; www.sustrans.org.uk.
Landmark, Carrbridge (10 miles) – rock climbing, flume rides, treetop walk and some educational stuff craftily dressed up as fun; April to October/November to March adult £10.55/£3.45, child £8.25/£2.50; open daily 10am–5/6/7pm depending on time of year; 01479 841613; www.landmarkpark.co.uk.

open	April to October
tiny campsites' rating	★ ★ ★
friendliness	☺ ☺ ☺
cost	BP ££, Couple £££, Family £££££

There are some campsites that you arrive at and immediately think, 'Ah yes, this is how it should be done'. The Lazy Duck is just such a one. From its hammocks strung across trees to its butterfly-filled wildflower garden, it could hardly be more relaxed or aesthetically pleasing if it tried.

Just outside the village of Nethy Bridge, on the edge of the Cairngorms, and half a mile up a forest track, Lazy Duck's campsite is in a small glade guarded by a brigade of red squirrels and equipped with a chimenea and log seats for communal evening gatherings (for the campers; not the squirrels). Only four small tents are allowed on the site, so do check on the website for availability before you email to book.

The list of attractive features at the Lazy Duck is a long one and includes the bush shower (commune with nature the Australian way); the open-ended campers' shelter with its tea-light lanterns on the tables; the walk out to the juniper moor to view CairnGorm mountain; and the numerous eponymous, exotic and, it has to be said, lazy ducks.

Just to top it off, if you arrive by bicycle or on foot the owners not only guarantee to fit you in somewhere (if you haven't booked and the campsite's full), but you'll be greeted in the traditional Moroccan manner: with a mixture of green and mint tea from a Berber teapot and a bowl of trail mix (okay, the Moroccans usually just go for fruit, but let's not be pernickety) absolutely free. Fab.

Croft Road
Lochcarron
Ross-shire
IV54 8YA

Iain Macray
01520 722898
dunrovinjo@tiscali.co.uk
Landranger: 24/25 (NG 906 400)

THE BASICS
Size: ½ acre.
Pitches: 21 (6 hard standing).
Terrain: Flat terraces.
Shelter: Yes.
View: Loch Carron.
Waterside: The shore is a minute's walk away.
Electric hook-ups: 6.
Noise/Light/Olfactory pollution: No.

THE FACILITIES
Loos: 2U. **Showers**: 2U (free).
Other facilities: Washing-up area, washing machine (£1.50), Lindy's Laundry in Lochcarron can dry clothes if it's raining; NB there is no CDP.
Stuff for children: No.
Recycling: Glass, tins, paper.

THE RULES
Dogs: Yes, under control. **Fires**: No open fires; BBQs off grass. **Other**: No.

PUB LIFE
Rockvilla Hotel, Lochcarron (100 metres) – very convenient, with the added bonus of tartan carpets; open 4–11pm 7D; food served 5–9pm 7D; 01520 722379; www.rockvilla-hotel.co.uk.
Or try the similarly genteel **Lochcarron Hotel** – for a later night; open 11am–'late' 7D; food served 12–8:45pm 7D; 01520 722226; www.lochcarronhotel.com.

SHOP
Lochcarron Food Centre (Spar and PO; ¼ mile) – multi-award-winning (rejoice!) large convenience store and off licence; open Mon–Fri 8am–7pm, Sat 8:30am–7pm, Sun 10am–4pm; 01520 722209.

THERE AND AWAY
Train station: Strathcarron (3 miles) – Inverness to Kyle of Lochalsh line. Buses go from Strathcarron to Lochcarron, or hop in a taxi (Lochcarron Taxis; 07774 499767).

OUT AND ABOUT
Strome Castle, Stromemore (3½ miles) – the romantic lochside ruins of a 15th-century stronghold (captured and unceremoniously blown up by the Mackenzies of Kintail in 1602), with splendid views down Loch Carron; free; always open; tinyurl.com/ytesbp.
Attadale Gardens, nr Strathcarron (4¾ miles) – 20 acres of gardens created by Baron Schroder in the 19th century and completely reworked by artist Nicky Macpherson, with terrific views out to Skye; adult £4.50, child £1; open daily April to October 10am–5:30pm; 01520 722603; www.attadalegardens.com.
Plockton (18 miles) – a remarkably pretty village at the far end of the loch and the setting for cult television series *Hamish MacBeth*; www.plockton.com.

open	early April to October
tiny campsites' rating	★ ★
friendliness	☺☺
cost	BP £, Couple ££, Family ££££

Highland wind, as any Highlander will tell you, is just, well, faster than any wind anywhere else in Britain. Therefore, should you come around the eastern tip of the tidal Loch Carron and be suddenly hit by a piledriver of a gale that sparks visions of having your tent/campervan/caravan unceremoniously picked up and dumped in the loch; then there's good news: the Wee Camp Site is sheltered by such a stout barrier of fir trees along its western edge that peace and tranquillity are guaranteed here.

Perched up on a slope above Lochcarron village, the site has been made possible by the creation of terraces, each large enough for four or five pitches; with the upper ones enjoying a glorious view over the loch to Ben Killilan, Sguman Coinntich (snow-capped for much of the year), copious waterfalls and the mountains of the Killilan Forest. This rather steals the glory from the vista to the rear – Glas Bheinn and other mountains beyond – which most campsite owners would kill to possess. The soil on the terraces is rather thin, but there are some stones underneath the trees to aid and abet with anchoring tent pegs (and you might even find some alpine strawberries while you're fetching them).

Lochcarron, a village spun out as thin as silk along the lochside, has a surprising number of shops and services for its size including a good café, a bistro and even a bank. It also boasts a dozen local Munros, and some excellent walking country (a book of routes is available at the tourist information centre).

Croft 9
Badrallach
Dundonnell
Ross-shire
IV23 2QP

Mick and Ali Stott
01854 633281
mail@badrallach.com
www.badrallach.com
OS Landranger: 19 (NH 066 917)

THE BASICS
Size: 4/5 acre.
Pitches: 19 (0 hard standing).
Terrain: Mainly gently sloping.
Shelter: Some pitches.
View: Mountains, waterfalls and sea loch.
Waterside: Little Loch Broom (300 metres to the shore via a footpath).
Electric hook-ups: 3.
Noise/Light/Olfactory pollution: Lights on around bothy for late-night loo trips.

THE FACILITIES
Loos: 2M 2W 1Disabled. **Showers**: 2U (free).
Other facilities: Kitchen (inc. washing-up area and fridge), washing line, table-tennis table. If not booked by a group, the bothy facilities can be used by campers: eating area, peat-burning stove, darts, board games, tourist info, small library and flash settee; NB no CDP.
Stuff for children: No.
Recycling: No.

THE RULES
Dogs: If well behaved (sheep in neighbouring fields).
Fires: Fire pits on half of pitches; BBQs off grass. **Other**: Only 3 campervans or caravans on site at any one time, prior booking essential.

PUB LIFE
Dundonnell Hotel (free house), nr Dundonnell (7½ miles) – choose either the Cocktail or the Broombeg Bar (and remind yourself that it's a very long walk to the nearest proper pub); open Mon–Sat 12–11pm, Sun till 10:30pm; food served 12–2pm 7D & Mon–Thur 6–8:30pm, Fri &

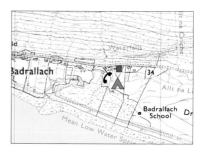

Sat till 9pm, Sun till 8pm; 01854 633204; www.dundonnellhotel.com.

SHOP
Dundonnell PO, nr Badcaul (14 miles) – well-stocked grocer's; open 8am–6pm; 01854 633208.

THERE AND AWAY
Train station: Garve (38 miles) – Inverness to Kyle of Lochalsh line. See facing page for onward transport options.

OUT AND ABOUT
An Teallach (8 miles) – 'Scotland's finest ridge walk', includes 2 Munros; 635-metre Beinn Ghobhlach (tinyurl.com/ycso43o) is just behind the campsite; and there's a beautiful 5-mile lochside stroll into the road-less off-grid community of Scoraig.
Gairloch Marine Life Centre (40 miles) – join an expert marine biologist on a 2-hour cruise to spot porpoises, whales, dolphins and basking sharks; adult £20, U18 £10; Easter to September trips at 10am, 12:30, 3 and 5pm; 01445 712636; www.porpoise-gairloch.co.uk.

open	All year
tiny campsites' rating	✳ ✳ ✳
friendliness	☺☺☺
cost	BP ££, Couple ££, Family £££

In a satisfyingly remote spot on the Scoraig Peninsula, with a most spectacular view – the ridge of An Teallach on the far side of Little Loch Broom dwarfing the few white houses beneath it – Badrallach offers campers the choice of a pitch in a small open field sloping towards the loch or one of handful hidden away in the gorse. Your neighbours may include pine martens, red deer, golden eagles, white-tailed sea eagles and red squirrels, so keep your eyes peeled.

If you fancy an active stay, there's a fantastic range of equipment for hire from the site at very reasonable rates including mountain bikes, a blo-kart (a three-wheeled sail board), a power kite (basically a kite far larger than nature intended), a tandem kayak, two single kayaks, an inflatable 6 h.p.-boat and even a Shetland whilly (a wooden clinker-built sail boat).

The nearest shop is a hilly 14 miles away, but milk, bread and organic fruit and veg (in season) can be bought on site, while other inhabitants of the township will also happily supply free-range eggs and a wider range of your five-a-day. Furthermore, the owners run a collection service 'for the cost of the fuel and a tip' from Ullapool, Garve or Inverness. Alternatively, you can catch the Westerbus service (www. ullapool.com/westerbus.rtf) from Inverness (Mon/Wed/Fri) to within seven miles of the campsite and get picked up from there.

Throw into the mix a wonderfully well-turned-out gaslit bothy to hide in should the weather turn and you've got a truly exceptional campsite.

Inver Caravan Park
Houstry Road
Dunbeath
Caithness
KW6 6EH

Rhona Gwillim
01593 731441
rhonagwillim@yahoo.co.uk
www.inver-caravan-park.co.uk
Landranger: 11/17 (ND 166 299)

THE BASICS
Size: 1 acre.
Pitches: 17 (9 hard standing).
Terrain: Gradual slope.
Shelter: Partial and not from east.
View: The North Sea (through the trees) and Dunbeath Castle.
Waterside: The sea is a field away, across the road.
Electric hook-ups: 17.
Noise/Light/Olfactory pollution: Some traffic on the A9.

THE FACILITIES
Loos: 2U. **Showers**: 2U (free).
Other facilities: Washing machine, tumble-dryer, 70-metre washing line.
Stuff for children: No.
Recycling: Everything.

THE RULES
Dogs: Under control. **Fires**: No open fires; BBQs off grass (stones on site). **Other**: No.

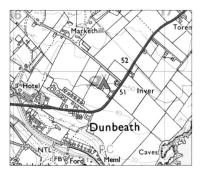

7:30am–1pm & 2–6pm (Thur & Fri till 7pm), Sat 7:30am–7pm, Sun 7:30am–1pm & 2–5pm; 01593 731217.

PUB LIFE
The Inver Arms, just a minute's walk down the A9, used to be one of the least attractive buildings in Scotland, with décor to match. Happily, it was taken over in late 2008 and is being given a complete overhaul including a new name, the **Bay Owl**, and now booking is essential; open 11am–midnight 7D; food served Mon–Fri 12–2:30pm & 5–8pm; Sat 12–3pm & 5–8:30pm, Sun 12:30–3pm & 5–7:30pm; 01593 731356.

SHOP
P & N (Spar), Dunbeath (½ mile) – small convenience store; open Mon–Fri

THERE AND AWAY
Train station: Helmsdale (16 miles) – Inverness to Wick/Thurso line. From Helmsdale bus no. X99 stops at Dunbeath.

OUT AND ABOUT
Dunbeath Heritage Centre (¾ mile) – an absorbing exploration of the history of this small village, from ancient rune-inscribed stones to present day matters; adult £2, child free; open daily April to September 10am–5pm, October to March 11am–3pm; 01593 731233; www.dunbeath-heritage.org.uk.
Dunbeath Strath and Broch, Dunbeath (½ mile to start of walk) – stride along Dunbeath Water up to a 2,000-year-old Broch (tower), a high gorge and standing stones; free; always open; www.dunbeath-heritage.org.uk/trail.html.

open	All year
tiny campsites' rating	★ ★
friendliness	☺☺☺
cost	BP £, Couple £££, Family ££££

High on a hill above the village of Dunbeath, this site looks out to the sea with one eye, and inland towards hills and mountains with the other.

It should be said straight off that the campsite is located slap-bang on the A9 as it cruises towards Thurso in the far north-east, but traffic around here is a whole lot sparser than that experienced further south, and at night becomes so light as to be almost unnoticeable. Indeed, you're more likely to be woken by the early morning calls of curlews than by anything speeding north. Facilities-wise, the loos and showers have undergone a complete refurbishment and now, aside from being all shiny and new, boast under-floor heating too.

Just 36 miles short of John o'Groats, the site is very handy for a last or first night on the End-to-End route, as well as for trips to the Orkneys from Scrabster (28 miles), or a visit to Whaligoe Steps (13 miles) for a look at Britain's oddest harbour (it has always been laughably dangerous).

Despite its self-designation as a caravan park, this site is just as welcoming to campers as caravanners, and the former have the pick of the best pitches up at the top end of the field. There are also very preferential rates given to backpackers and cyclists, making this one of the best value campsites for walkers and riders in Scotland. Furthermore, anyone staying for a week gets the seventh night free. Result!

Melvich
Sutherland
KW14 7YJ

Ian and Marilyn Fling

01641 531282

mazfling@tinyworld.co.uk

www.halladaleinn.co.uk

Landranger: 10 (NC 887 640)

THE BASICS
Size: ⁹/₁₀ acre.
Pitches: 19 (11 hard standing).
Terrain: Gently sloping.
Shelter: Some pitches in lee of pub.
View: Fields, the valley of the River Halladale and the North Sea.
Waterside: A 10-minute walk to the beach.
Electric hook-ups: 11.
Noise/Light/Olfactory pollution: Music from the pub goes on until late; streetlights at night.

THE FACILITIES
Loos: 1M 2W. **Showers**: 1M 1W (free).
Other facilities: Washing-up area, washing machine, tumble-dryer, 2 picnic tables.
Stuff for children: No.
Recycling: No.

THE RULES
Dogs: Yes.
Fires: No open fires; BBQ provided (it's an oil drum sliced in half). **Other**: No.

PUB LIFE
Halladale Inn (free house; 20 metres) – the popular restaurant specialises in locally sourced food; open Mon–Thur 11am–11pm, Fri 11–1am, Sat till midnight, Sun 12–11pm; food served 12–8pm 7D.

SHOP
The West End PO, Portskerra (1¼ miles) – basic foodstuffs; open Mon–Sat 9am–6pm; 01641 531219.

THERE AND AWAY
Train station: Forsinard (15 miles) – Inverness to Wick/Thurso line. Take a

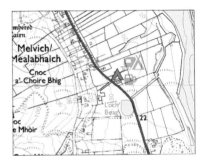

taxi from the station as public transport options are few and far between.

OUT AND ABOUT
Strathnaver Museum, Bettyhill (14 miles) – housed in the former church of St Columba, the museum takes visitors on a tour, from Strathnaver's numinous past all the way to the Highland Clearances; adult £2, child 50p, U5 free; open April to October Mon–Sat 10am–5pm; 01641 521418; www.strathnavermuseum.org.uk.

Forsinard Nature Reserve (13 miles) – wet bogs aren't, perhaps, humankind's favourite terrain, but there's plenty of wildlife that won't give them the cold shoulder. At Forsinard there's a chance of spying greenshanks, hen harriers, golden plovers, dunlin and the odd golden eagle; otters in the river or bog pools; and herds of red deer; free; open daily April to October 9am–6pm; 01955 602596; tinyurl.com/ye263u8.

open	All year
tiny campsites' rating	★ ★
friendliness	☺☺
cost	BP £, Couple ££, Family ££££

There can be few campsites in Britain that are more happily situated than this one next to Melvich's Halladale Inn on the not-quite-as-wild-as-you-might-imagine north coast of Scotland. Virtually all the pitches here enjoy views of sheep-filled fields that tumble down to the River Halladale as it makes its final lurch into the sea.

Campervanners and caravanners will enjoy the site's brand-new fast-draining gravelly section, while campers will be pleased to get on to the grass beyond to savour the view. The facilities are clean and welcoming and the pub is not only open all day, but serves food for eight straight hours of it.

The beach at Halladale Bay – a 10-minute walk down through those same sheep-filled fields – is simply captivating. Perhaps it's due to the sand dunes that pile up behind the beach, or it could be the oystercatchers, ringed plovers and curlews that flit past and up the clear shallow river, while cuckoos and wood pigeons lend their calls to the aural backdrop. You know you're only a hop and a step from a pub and the coastal road and civilisation and everything, but it does really feel like you've entered some enchanted seaside wilderness, which is perhaps why it also appeals to surfers (well, that and the waves, probably).

If you feel a need to seek out pleasures further afield, Orkney can be reached from Scrabster (16 miles) by ferry, while the little village of Tongue (26 miles) and its ruined castle are also worth a visit.

North Shawbost
Isle of Lewis
HS2 0BQ

Iain Macaulay

01851 710504

eileanfraoich@btinternet.com

eileanfraoich.co.uk

OS Landranger: 8/13 (NB 256 463)

THE BASICS
Size: ½ acre.
Pitches: 10 (3 hard standing).
Terrain: Flat.
Shelter: Some protection from southerly winds.
View: A glimpse of the sea through the trees.
Waterside: No.
Electric hook-ups: 6.
Noise/Light/Olfactory pollution: Exterior lights on buildings.

THE FACILITIES
Loos: 2M 2W 1Disabled. **Showers**: 1M 1W (20p for '2 min.').
Other facilities: Kitchen (inc. washing-up area, gas hob, fridge and toaster), dining area, laundry taken in, payphone, hairdryer, CDP.
Stuff for children: There's a playing field right next door with a football pitch, and for budding Olympians a long-jump pit and a shot-put circle (shots not provided).
Recycling: Glass, bottles, tins, organic waste.

THE RULES
Dogs: On leads; an exercise area is provided. **Fires**: No open fires; bricks available for BBQs off ground.
Other: In order not to upset local people, no washing is to be hung out on a Sunday.

PUB LIFE
The Doune Braes Hotel (free house), Carloway (7 miles) – fairly standard hotel bar with restaurant, but in a terrifically scenic location; open Mon–Sat 12–11pm, Sun 12:30–9pm: food served Mon–Sat 12–8:30pm, Sun till 7:30pm; 01851 643252.

SHOP
Butt View Stores, South Bragar (1¾ miles) – basic foodstuffs, some hardware and the sort of name that ensured it was bullied at school; open Mon–Fri 9:30am–8pm, Sat 10am–9pm; 01851 710514.

THERE AND AWAY
Ferry Terminal: Stornoway (19 miles) – Caledonian MacBrayne ferries (08000 665000; www.calmac.co.uk) to/from Ullapool on the mainland. Bus no. W2 from Stornoway stops in Shawbost.

OUT AND ABOUT
Shawbost Museum (100 metres) – a look at local life down the ages; open April to September Mon–Sat 11am–4pm; 01851 710797.
The Black House, Arnol (7½ miles) – a traditional Lewis thatched house kept exactly as it was when abandoned in 1966, along with a furnished 1920s white house and some locally made crafts; adult £2.50, child £1.25; open April to September Mon–Sat 9:30am–5:30pm, till 4:30pm October to March; 01851 710395; tinyurl.com/ylk4s6o.

open	May to October
tiny campsites' rating	★ ★
friendliness	☺☺
cost	BP £, Couple ££, Family £££

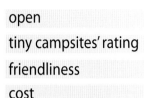

If prizes were awarded for sprawling, the village of Shawbost ('Siabost' in Gaelic) would never have to worry about owning an empty trophy-cabinet. Its houses straddle the coast road so interminably that anyone approaching Eilean Fraoich from the north could be forgiven for imagining that they might never arrive.

If and when they do, they will discover a campsite that is very far removed from the rough and rugged Lewisian landscape that surrounds it. Tent pegs slide into an immaculately kept lawn beside a neat, modern bungalow. The facilities are spotless, while the kitchen and dining room are not only very welcome (since it can get very breezy here indeed), but are so café-like that when you bustle about preparing your dinner you can have fun pretending you're a chef who has just opened up an exclusive Hebridean eatery, if you like.

Milk and gas, that ever-winning combination, can be purchased on site, as can newspapers if ordered the day before, which is a rare luxury. In cold weather, the owner will even supply blankets on request.

The tariff here is based on the size of tent rather than the number of people in it, so if you can shoehorn your family/friends/colleagues into a two-man job, so much the better. The sea is but a quarter of a mile away, although the nearest access to it requires a 20-minute stroll, during which you can all get some feeling back into your limbs.

A Word for Walkers

There's something pleasingly visceral about backpacking. It's just you, the outdoors, a few victuals and a simple shelter for the night. No matter that your provisions are a vacuum-packed bag of dehydrated vegetable curry and that your shelter sports the latest developments in ultra-lightweight rip-stop trilaminate, there's still an element of being at one with nature that is hard to beat.

Furthermore, campsite owners love walkers. Maybe they sense that this is somehow 'as it ought to be', or perhaps they just like the fact that walkers have no vehicles that may need towing off the field if it pours with rain. Whatever the reason, time and time again I've been told by campsite owners, 'We don't turn away hikers, no matter how full we might be – we always find a corner for them somewhere.' One proprietor informed me that she'd even had walkers staying in her garden when her camping field was full. That's not to say that it's advisable to rock up anywhere and hope, of course, but it's nice to know that there are plenty of people out there who will take pity on you if you happen to wander in on spec, blistered and hunchbacked from a long day's hike.

When I don my walking boots, one of my favourite destinations is Foxhole Bottom (p66) on the South Downs. Aside from being one of relatively few camping grounds on the South Downs Way, it's also handy for the Vanguard Way, a 66-mile path that starts, rather unpromisingly, at East Croydon station, but then charts an extraordinarily diverse and surprisingly picturesque route down to Newhaven on the Sussex coast.

Further west, anyone who spends a night or two at Porthllisky Farm (p140) and who doesn't feel an urgent desire to explore St David's Peninsula on foot should have their pulse checked at once to make sure their heart's still functioning. Meanwhile, the five-mile hike from Badrallach (p178) along Little Loch Broom to the isolated and road-less community at Scoraig (they get around by boat) is one guaranteed to enthuse even the most reluctant of walkers.

While all the campsites in this book make splendid bases for a day's wandering about, there are some that offer the added bonus of lying close to, or right on, a long-distance footpath. Thus, for those planning a longer walk, here's a list of signed trails near featured campsites:

Trail	No.	Campsite
Beacons Way	59	Little Oasis
Cleveland Way	50	Park Farm
Coast to Coast Walk	49	Hollins Farm
Cumbria Way	45	Birchbank Farm
Cumbrian Coastal Way	45	Birchbank Farm
Fen Rivers Way	32	Braham Farm
Monarch's Way	19	Gumber Farm
Mortimer Trail	37	The Buzzards
Norfolk Coast Path	31	Scaldbeck Cottage
Offa's Dyke Path	35	The Bridge Inn
	59	Little Oasis
	63	Ty Maen Farm
Ouse Valley Way	32	Braham Farm
Pembrokeshire Coast Path	54	Porthllisky Farm
Pennine Way	51	Highside Farm
Sandstone Trail	40	Quarryfield
Severn Way	12	Rectory Farm
South Downs Way	19	Gumber Farm
	21	Foxhole Bottom
South West Coast Path	1	Broad Meadow House
	2	Dennis Farm
	3	Scadghill Farm
	6	Millslade
	9	California Cottage
Southern Upland Way	67	The Ken Bridge Hotel
Speyside Way	70	The Lazy Duck
Sussex Border Path	20	Evergreen Farm
Thames Path	16	Rushey Lock
	17	Pinkhill Lock
	18	Cookham Lock
Vanguard Way	21	Foxhole Bottom
Wye Valley Walk	61	Radnors End
	62	Trericket Mill
Wysis Way	13	Daneway Inn

A Word for Cyclists

There's very little to compare in this life with the sensation of having an open road before you, a bicycle beneath whose pedals whirr round at the slightest pressure and a friendly wind at your back. All you need to add is a jaunty whistle, a couple of panniers and a tiny tent, and the world is yours.

As mentioned elsewhere, I visited all 75 campsites in this book by bicycle – an old-school Falcon Oxford tourer I bought second-hand 10 years ago for the princely sum of £28 – and can thus confirm not only that they are accessible on two wheels, but that getting to them can be an immensely pleasurable business, especially if you let the train do most of the work first (see Taking the Train, p190).

I felt, therefore, that I would take the liberty of passing on a few insider tips to those readers who fancy visiting one or more of the campsites in this book *à bicyclette*.

For the novice or occasional cyclist

If you are the sort of cyclist who is not naturally wedded to the saddle, it's always a good idea to have a quick peek at a map to see if your campsite of choice is surrounded by contours. Cycling 20 miles on the flat of the Fens is a very different matter to pedalling the same distance in humpy-bumpy Devon. I once made the mistake of taking my girlfriend, who was brought up in ironing-board flat Cambridgeshire, for a ride in Northumberland that I had assumed would be fairly straightforward and take us no longer than 90 minutes. When we arrived at our destination four hours later after some absolute killer hills I had lost a considerable number of hard-won boyfriend points.

So, if you were to cycle to Sweet Meadows (p30), for instance, you would be advised not to start off from Exeter as there's an almighty hill between the two. However, Yeoford station, a little to the north-west, lends itself to a route via far more manageable ascents. Likewise, head for

Millslade (p32) via Lynmouth and you will encounter the thigh-punishing Countisbury Hill, which starts off at a gradient of 1:4 and doesn't get much easier for the next two miles.

If even the prospect of a gentle incline brings you out in a cold sweat there is still hope – just book yourself in to any of the East Anglian sites (see pages 78–91) and breeze on in.

For more experienced cyclists

The more practised cyclists among you will no doubt be chafing at such advice and are probably even now making a mental note to approach Millslade via Lynmouth just for the sheer joy of taking on a hill worthy of the name. If you find yourself in this category, allow me to recommend Gwersyll Maes-y-Bryn (p160), a three-mile climb from Llanrwst, and Badrallach (p178), one of the remotest sites in the country and one with a real sense of destination, especially when you look down on it from the top of the final hill and realise that all there is between you and it is a long exhilarating drop.

Something for everyone

You'll find a Cyclists' category on p17 listing all the campsites that are either located in countryside that cries out to be cycled through or are close to designated trails. To get you started, here are the cycle paths and mountain-bike circuits that are easily accessible from campsites in this book:

Black and White Trail	37	The Buzzards
C2C	52	The Old Vicarage
Camel Trail	2	Dennis Farm
Deers Leap Park mountain bike trails	20	Evergreen Farm
Forest of Bowland cycle routes	43	Crawshaw Farm
Glastonbury & Wells National Byway Loop	7	Bridge Farm
Holderness National Byway Loop	47	Elmtree Farm
Kennet and Avon Canal cycle path	11	Church Farm
Killer Loop mountain bike circuit	60	Castle Inn
National Cycle Route No. 7	70	The Lazy Duck
Seven Stanes mountain bike trails	67	The Ken Bridge Hotel
	68	Glenmidge Smithy

Taking the Train

One of the many joys of camping is that it allows us to wave a fond farewell to the trappings of everyday modern life. For a brief period we allow ourselves a respite from work, television, central heating, emails and, if we enter into the spirit of things, mobile phones too. It can also be very satisfying to forego the stress and bother of driving to a chosen holiday destination in favour of getting there by public transport.

Contrary to popular opinion, the railway system in Britain is pretty efficient – in the months I spent roving around the country researching this book, I didn't experience a single cancellation and, miraculously, the only time a train was really late coincided with the one occasion on which I'd misjudged the distance from a campsite to a station and got in horribly late too.

I took my bike on the train wherever I went but, if you're not a cyclist, the vast majority of the campsites can still be reached from their nearest station by bus or, in some cases, simply by walking (see Easy Public Transport, p19). Planning the journey is also now a lot simpler and more straightforward with the advent of such websites as Transport Direct (www.transportdirect.info).

However, it must be admitted that the proliferation of train companies that criss-cross the nation nowadays is apt to cause a certain amount of confusion. Therefore, to help make things a bit clearer, there follows a brief guide to the rail companies that serve the campsites featured in this book.

ARRIVA TRAINS WALES
Network: ATW covers the whole of Wales and has lines reaching out from the principality to Manchester, Birmingham and Cheltenham. The Wales Flexi-Rover ticket allows passengers to travel over the entire ATW network, the Ffestiniog and Welsh Highland railways, and most scheduled bus services.
Website: www.arrivatrainswales.co.uk

Ticket sales: 08709 000773 (Welsh Language service: 08456 040500)

CROSS COUNTRY
Network: A main line running from Cornwall to Aberdeen with routes off to Manchester, Reading and Bournemouth.
Website: www.crosscountrytrains.co.uk
Ticket sales: 08448 110124

EAST COAST
Network: Stretching up the spine of Britain from London King's Cross, to the East Midlands, Yorkshire and Humberside, North East England and Scotland all the way north to Aberdeen and Inverness.
Website: www.eastcoast.co.uk
Ticket sales: 08457 225225

EAST MIDLAND TRAINS
Network: An extensive service radiating out from Nottingham to take in London, Leicester, Crewe, Matlock, Liverpool, Sheffield, York, Skegness and Norwich among others.
Website: www.eastmidlandstrains.co.uk
Ticket sales: 08457 125678

FIRST GREAT WESTERN
Network: Includes south Wales, the West Country to the far end of Cornwall, the Cotswolds, and large parts of Southern England, with frequent services to and from London.
Website: www.firstgreatwestern.co.uk
Ticket sales: 08457 000125

NATIONAL EXPRESS EAST ANGLIA
Network: Covers Cambridgeshire, Norfolk, Suffolk, much of Essex and some of Hertfordshire, with trains leaving from London.
Website: www. nationalexpresseastanglia.com
Ticket sales: 08456 007245

NORTHERN
Network: Spreads over the whole of northern England from Crewe, Stoke, Buxton and Nottingham in the south, to Carlisle and Newcastle in the north.
Website: www.northernrail.org
Ticket sales: 08450 000125

SCOTRAIL
Network: ScotRail runs trains on all Scottish routes and boasts a sleeper service linking London with northern Scotland.
Website: www.scotrail.co.uk
Ticket sales: 08457 550033

SOUTH WEST TRAINS
Network: From London to Portsmouth, Weymouth, Exeter, Reading and the Isle of Wight.
Website: www.southwesttrains.co.uk
Ticket sales: 08456 000650

SOUTHERN
Network: Covers the counties to the south of London including Surrey, East and West Sussex, along with some of Kent and Hampshire.
Website: www.southernrailway.com
Ticket sales: 08451 272920

TRANSPENNINE EXPRESS
Network: As the name suggests, TE covers routes across the Pennines from Liverpool, Blackpool and Barrow across to Hull, Cleethorpes and Scarborough. They also run services up the east coast to Newcastle and the west coast to Glasgow and Edinburgh.
Website: www.tpexpress.co.uk (check out the bouncing rabbits on the interactive network map)
Ticket sales: 08457 000125

USEFUL INFO
National Rail Enquires: 08457 484950 (24 hours); www.nationalrail.co.uk.

A to B Magazine's Bike/Rail Page is full of excellent information on when and where you can travel on trains, buses and ferries with a bicycle: www.atob.org.uk/Bike-Rail.html.

AUTHOR ACKNOWLEDGEMENTS

I'd like to proffer my heartfelt thanks to all those who helped make my life sweeter in some way or other during the research for this book, and in particular: Rensie and Damian 'bassman' Basher; Deb, Sam and Jethro Best; Robert Stanford; Henrietta Evans; Cecilia at Pandy; James Bladen and Vanna Lundin; Julie and Chris Hindley; the van Zijl family; Ros Loten; Carey and Dave Watson; Chloë and Kate; Warren and Denhy for their fab mango and chile salad; Sara and Estelle with their slightly less than fab incinerated marshmallows; Dave Dukes; Gail and Danny Freeman-Dinner; Elaine at The Buzzards; Thomas & June McMillan; Rin and Cobby, purveyors of the finest vegetarian jelly; Michael Breckon at The National Byway; Carl and Viv Palmer; Tara at Middle Ninfa; Kim, Nick, Freddy and Jet; Clive and Edwin; Ellie Banks at First Great Western; Carla Rinaldi at ScotRail; John Gelson and Paul Williams at National Express East Coast; Carolyn Watson and Clare Conlin at Northern Rail; Chris Hudson at Southern Rail; Emma Knight at Southwest Trains and East Midland Trains; Maggie Abbett at Arriva Trains Wales; Ellen Rossiter at National Express East Anglia; David Mallender at Transpennine Express; Lee West at Cross Country; Iain Crawford at Vango; Rob Cater at Decathlon; the staff at Bethnal Green library; The Guildensterns, and The Boys and Ellie and Apricot.

Special thanks to Elisabeth Whitebread for her help with research and for her general forbearance.

And, finally, I would like to express my gratitude to the scores of campsite owners who welcomed me warmly no matter which of my two highly attractive post-cycling states I arrived in: soaked to the skin or wreathed in sweat. It's very much appreciated.

For the record, the tents I use are a Quechua T2 ultralight pro and, when I want to go ultra-ultralight, Vango's Helium 100. The former is a doddle to pitch, is very roomy inside and, for an ultralight tent, is very cheap. The latter finds its way into my rucksack when I need something really small and light – it's the same weight as a bag of sugar and folds away into almost nothing.

Lastly, for those who take pleasure in finding out such things, the vast majority of the photographs in this book were taken on a Fuji F200EXR. Other cameras used were also Fujis – an F50fd and an S5500. So now you know.

Tiny Campsites
Researched, written and photographed by:
Dixe Wills
Publisher: Jonathan Knight
Managing Editor: Sophie Dawson
Design: Dave Jones
Proofreader: Nikki Sims
PR: Carol Farley
Marketing: Shelley Bowdler

Published by: Punk Publishing, 3 The Yard, Pegasus Place, London SE11 5SD
Distributed by: Portfolio Books, 2nd Floor, Westminster House, Kew Road, Richmond, Surrey TW9 2ND

All photographs © Dixe Wills except the following (all reproduced with permission): p5, br © Mick Stott/Badrallach; front cover flap & pages 20, 38, 58, 78, 92, 112, 138 & 166 © Andy Stothert; p181 © Colette & Christian Gobeli; p185 © Iain Macaulay/Eilean Fraoich.

OS Maps created by Lovell Johns Limited. Based upon Ordnance Survey digital map data © Crown Copyright 2010 Licence Number 43368U. All rights reserved.

The publishers and author have done their best to ensure the accuracy of all information in *Tiny Campsites*. However, they can accept no responsibility for any injury, loss, or inconvenience sustained by anyone as a result of information contained in this book.

Punk Publishing takes its environmental responsibilities seriously. This book has been printed on paper made from renewable sources and we continue to work with our printers to reduce our overall environmental impact.

We hope you've enjoyed reading *Tiny Campsites* and that it's inspired you to explore Britain's best littlest sites. The campsites featured are a personal selection chosen by the author. None of the campsites has paid a fee for inclusion, nor was one requested, so you can be sure of an objective choice of sites and honest descriptions. Dixe Wills visited hundreds of campsites to find this selection, but it hasn't been possible for him to visit every British campsite. So, if you know of a special place that's an acre or under that you think should be included, please send an email to tinycampsites@punkpublishing.co.uk telling us the name and location of the campsite, some contact details and why it's so special. We'll credit all useful contributions in the next edition, and senders of the best emails will receive a complimentary copy.